The Countryside at War

The COUNTRYSIDE at War

Ian Grant Nicholas Maddren

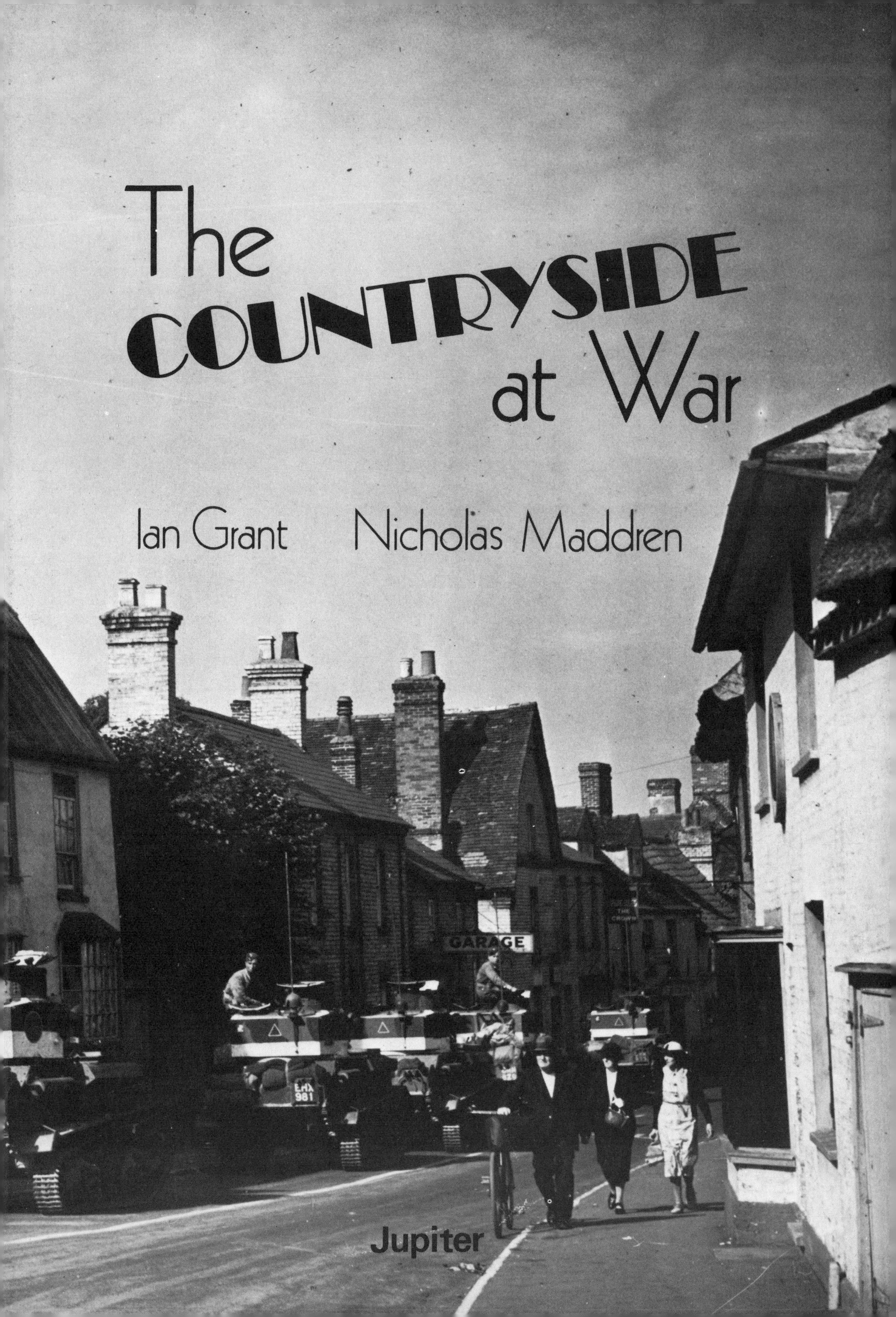

Jupiter

Jupiter Books (London) Ltd,
167 Hermitage Road, Harringay, London N4 1LZ.

First published 1975

Produced by Campion Design.

The Countryside at War © Jupiter Books (London) Ltd 1975
SBN 904041 28 X

Set in 'Monotype' Plantin 110 by
The Lancashire Typesetting Company Limited, Bolton.

Printed and bound by R. J. Acford Ltd., Industrial Estate, Chichester.

Contents

Introduction

In the First World War, Britain had come close to surrender as the German blockade slowly cut off food supplies. In the Second, the Battle of the Atlantic was fought for the same supremacy of the seas.

Shipping was vital to survival, since before the war Britain imported huge amounts of food. British farms themselves were in large measure geared towards cattle-farming and the manufacture of dairy produce, which was too expensive for almost a third of the British population to afford.

The British Government was faced with two massive agricultural problems: how to make up for the enormous shortfall of cereals, vegetables and meat which, under severe conditions of blockade could no longer be imported; and how to distribute the whole range of foodstuffs essential to a population about to be faced with the nervous and physical strain of a war which might well last for years, at a price which would not be economically ruinous both to producer and consumer. The farmer's difficulties were not lessened by the fact that farm workers were called up into the Forces; that his family might be housing and feeding extra mouths in the form of evacuees; that he himself might be involved in long hours of Home Guard duty; that in the south-east of England he was often forced to work under a fierce storm of machine-gun bullets, bombs and shells from enemy aircraft and guns.

The story of the British farmers' wartime labours is often outwardly undramatic. The military conflict across the fields of Britain which a German invasion could have brought on never materialised. But agriculture cannot be geared up for war production in the same way that a factory can be re-tooled, or new premises built and production set in motion. The farming year has to run its course, and only once a year can the course be changed. So the farmers had to run a slow but urgent race against time, to keep Britain alive in the face of the German blockade until the fortune of war turned in the Allies' favour – if it ever did.

Ian Grant
Plumstead, London, May 1975

The Empty Fields

During the First World War, Britain was almost starved into surrender as German submarines sank increasing numbers of merchant ships, many of which brought food into the country. To relieve the distress, the Government looked to the farmers to produce more food. Encouraged by the introduction of a system of guaranteed prices for farm produce, and the regulation of wage rates, farmers and their workers made gigantic efforts to compensate for the shortage of food supplies – efforts in which they were largely successful.

The National Government of the late 1930s, aware of the possibility of another war, looked back to this example and began to introduce measures to step up food production before war brought on the crisis of food shortage yet again. But the fact that they had to introduce special measures, that farmers were again in need of official encouragement to work the land to its full capacity, shows up the failure of successive Governments, between the two wars, to keep faith with the farming community which had made such great efforts in 1917 and 1918. During the 1920s the industry was allowed to decline and was in poor shape when the slump of the early 1930s hit the trade of the industrialised nations and sent the prices of all commodities, including agricultural produce, quickly downwards. Farmers were amongst the worst sufferers in the depression, for historical economic reasons.

For half a century or more before the outbreak of the First World War, control of the production and distribution of food had gradually passed out of the hands of individual farmers to wholesale food distributors and their financial backers. Until the beginning of the nineteenth century, farmers had been able to expect a standard price for their produce – as was reintroduced in the First World War, in the Second World War and, in some instances, in the present day.

On heavy soil and steep ground three horses yoked together were needed to draw a plough. In the distance their successor, the tractor, works a neighbouring field.

Women's Land Army, 1918 Girls of the original WLA bagging grain newly threshed, which had stood in ricks since the 1917 harvest season.

brought, the fortunes of the political rulers of the nation – was built upon exporting manufactured goods.

To the people who directed the nation's affairs, it was obvious that Britain's exporting industries should be maintained and expanded. The countries which supplied raw materials also supplied food at prices cheaper than those farmers at home could afford to ask in order to earn a decent living. The movement away from the countryside to the industrial cities enabled more exports to be produced; more exports were sold in exchange for cheap food from abroad; cheap food put more home farmers in difficulties and drove more men and their families into the cities. Agriculture became generally associated with a state of poverty and a feeling of resentment on the part of agricultural workers, who were less considered and less understood by the administrators of the country's affairs as the nineteenth century came to an end. The economic principles of free trade and *laissez faire*, allowing 'market forces' to adjust buying and selling prices without any form of government intervention, hastened the decline.

By 1914, the agricultural industry had lost half the farmers and farmworkers it had had a century before. Large areas of land were no longer cultivated, arable land was turned into pasture land and fields lost their fertility. Some farmers, energetic and eternally optimistic, who had good land, managed to make a living; others, who had an additional source of income, were able to support themselves with its aid. But they were the lucky ones – many more failed to survive.

The crisis of the First World War was so sharp that it produced a public policy which was the reverse of all that had been accepted administrative doctrine for two generations or more. The German submarine blockade had been underrated. By 1916 food supplies were becoming dangerously low and deliveries from abroad erratic. The lack of a rationing scheme until the last year of the war meant that the burden of food shortage fell heavily on the poorest sections of the population. Hesitantly, since agriculture had become, by tradition, a third-rate industry, the Government looked at measures to encourage an increase in agricultural production.

The farmer's risk – the uncertainty of the price he would receive for his goods at the market – was reduced by the institution of a system of guaranteed prices for farm produce. If a farmer knew that he would be certain to receive a definite sum for his goods, he would be more likely to invest his time and money in their production. To encourage a workforce back to the land, a minimum wage for farm workers was agreed. Perhaps the most important incentives the Government offered were the promises they made regarding the status of the farming community after the war was over. Never again, it was claimed, would

At the same time, laws were repealed which had been in force for centuries, making dealing or gambling in food illegal. The entrepreneur was allowed into the system, paying one price for food bought from the farmer and receiving another from the customers to whom he sold it. The farmer became uncertain of the price he would get for his goods; in fact, the price fluctuated wildly. Sometimes he made a large profit; more often his return was poor and, for many, farming became a financially precarious way of life.

The instability of farming contributed to the steadily increasing flow of migrants from the countryside into the new industrial towns of England. The plight of the countryside worsened for the loss of labour; towns grew haphazardly and speculatively, to the neglect of the physical conditions and welfare of millions of people. The rise in importance of the towns turned the draining of countrymen out of the land into a vicious circle for farming as a whole. The towns were largely producing manufactured goods created out of imported raw materials. The wealth of nineteenth-century Britain – that is, the wealth of its industrialists, financiers, and, because of the power such wealth

A sunny Friday in Helmsley, Yorkshire, provides the setting for a peaceful pre-war market scene.

agriculture be allowed to fall into the state it had reached before the First World War. The broad promises were reinforced by legislation which gave them an air of permanence.

With the war over, people began to turn back to farming. Land prices rose, but the confidence engendered by government assurances that the value placed upon wartime agriculture would continue in peacetime persuaded many to raise large sums of money on mortgage in order to buy farms. In 1921, however, government policy was reversed once again. To the administrators of the nation, the best way of setting the country to rights again (as much socially as economically, since Britain was not in desperate financial straits) after the upheaval of the First World War was to attempt a reconstruction of a society closely resembling that of pre-war Britain, based on the same economic principles which had created Britain's industrial wealth. This involved a return to the Gold Standard, fixing the rate of exchange of the pound against other currencies, new encouragement for investment abroad, the export of manufactured goods and the import of raw materials and food. Once more, international trade rather then production for home

(or war) consumption was to be the prime feature of British economic policy. The legislation which had encouraged the return to British farming, the Corn Production Act, was repealed, since the Government felt it could no longer afford to guarantee the price of wheat and oats at the prevailing level of 1919, which was far higher than the market price in 1921. The grand and binding promises were repudiated and all but forgotten. Land prices fell, as did the price of farm produce. Farmers sank deeper into debt as the value of their land and the return on their capital declined. High hopes were choked, leaving a bitter sense of betrayal that the Government which had buoyed up the farming industry when the nation was in danger should have let them down harshly when the crisis was passed.

Farming was hit badly by the effects of the world economic slump which began in 1929. As manufacturing industries slowed to a halt and unemployment rose, lack of money in people's pockets led to a decline in demand for all goods, including food, despite its being essential to health and strength. The price of basic foodstuffs fell. By the economic principles of the time, if prices fell it was because the demand was low; if demand was low, there must be an excessive amount of that commodity on the market – the consequence, so it was thought, of over-production.

The legacy of nineteenth-century economics was still so current in the 1930s that food was considered by those who had the regulation of the distribution system and the ordering of wholesale markets to be simply another commercial commodity, rather than something basic to the sustenance of life itself. Consequently the regulation of supply and demand which had to take place in order to bring prices up again was based on calculations as to how much foodstuff should be allowed on to the market for prices to rise to a reasonable level of profit over the cost of production. Since over-production was thought to be the problem, imports of food were reduced to a level which, at other times, might have benefited farmers at home. At the same time the production of Britain's farmers was controlled so that less foodstuff should be brought to the market, thus stimulating demand and pushing up the price.

Control of production spelt yet more contraction in the farming industry. Millions of acres were allowed to go uncultivated and between the two World Wars more than 4 million acres of good arable land were either turned into pasture land or simply left to decay into untended scrub land. Above all, no thought was given to the requirements of the British people. A third of the population was undernourished, lacking money to buy enough food; the responsibility of a government

The tithe wars *above* were fought with a bitterness born of the sore distress which the Ecclesiastical Commissioners' administration of tithe collection had brought upon the agricultural community. *Below* arriving to harvest corn in fields from which a tithe payment was due to King's College, Cambridge.

Break for lunch from the slow, heavy work of ploughing on a dank autumn day.

to serve all the people of a nation, not simply a powerful minority, was ignored for the sake of the maintenance of the profits of food wholesalers and distributors. The prices that were fixed meant dearer food, increasing the burden on the poor and unemployed.

The food question was constantly studied during the 1930s, and gradually critical shortages of food were eased by the introduction of government subsidies and the rationalisation of distribution by setting up such institutions as the Milk and Potato Marketing Boards. Partially successful attempts to arrive at international agreements on export and import quotas of foodstuffs meant that, for Britain, home and Dominion-based producers of food benefited to some extent at the expense of foreign producers. The efforts of a succession of energetic Ministers of Agriculture, often against apathy or active opposition from other government departments, meant that over the 8 years before the outbreak of the Second World War, the agricultural community also received a number of indirect benefits. These included funds for the improvement of water supplies; livestock improvement schemes which encouraged the breeding of pedigree herds; and the provision of veterinary and pest control services.

The most far-reaching benefit was the mitigation of tithes, an ancient system of local ecclesiastical taxation, originally and for centuries a levy by the incumbent of each living of the established Church of a tenth of the produce of the agricultural land in his parish. Tithes-in-kind had given way to payments in cash during the nineteenth century. The payment was assessed as a proportion of the average price of crop values over a period of 7 years. Fluctuations in price caused alternating periods of distress and complacency for the farming community.

With farming buoyant at the end of the First World War, many tenants took over the freehold of farms, and with them the tithe rent-charges payable, from their former landlords. Incomes were good but, since it was foreseen that agricultural prices would probably decline a little, tithe rent-charges were fixed for a period of 6 years in order that undue distress should not arise as the charges, based on the 7-year average, descended less quickly than the farmers' incomes.

By 1921, it was obvious that this system was doomed to failure. Prices fell so fast that the tithe rent-charges became severely burdensome. In order to avoid parochial disturbances, which had occurred for the same reasons in past years, the collection of tithes was taken out of the hands of the individual clergymen on the spot and vested in an archaic institution known as

Queen Anne's Bounty, a body which attracted much opprobrium in the ensuing years. Queen Anne's Bounty acted on behalf of the Church of England not only in collecting tithe rent-charges but also in computing and demanding arrears of tithes which many clergymen, through inefficiency or leniency, had left uncollected. Throughout the 1920s and into the following decade many agricultural properties were forcibly split up and sold off in order to pay the tithe rent-charges. Farmers' goods were seized, domestic furniture carted off and families turned out of their houses. The farming community, going through severe times anyway, reacted vigorously. Demonstrations, some violent, gave rise to a Royal Commission which resulted, although not until 1936, in the Tithe Act, which finally removed the tithe rent-charge altogether.

The European situation as it developed in 1937 and 1938 gave the greatest impetus to the reorganisation of farming, this time with the intention of increasing production rather than raising the farmers' returns. Once more, as the danger of war threatened, farmers were encouraged to plough up more land, tempted, in April 1939, by a subsidy of £2 per acre and a guaranteed price for cereals they produced. As well as a policy of

increased food production, stores of the most important imported foods – wheat, sugar and whale oil, from which margarine was made – were built up. Contention between two opposing groups in the administrative departments of government, one for a policy of storage, one for increased production, meant that in the end a combination of both was adopted, to the detriment of the maximum efficiency of each. Stocks of lime, phosphates and other fertilisers were more easily managed and a reserve of tractors and mechanical implements was built up and concentrated mainly in the principal grain-growing area, the eastern counties of England. To iron out the financial bottlenecks in the distribution system, dealing and gambling in food was made illegal once more, after a period of 140 years.

Between the wars there were consistent advances in nutritional science, in the knowledge of the constituents of foodstuffs and their individual effects on human health. They formed the basis for the major improvement in the food administration of the Second World War over that of the First and for the hopes of many people who believed that agriculture should play a far more important role in national life. The study of the levels of consumption of different types of food revealed that cheap foods, as they were then, such as bread and sugar, were consumed in much the same amounts by the whole population. On the other hand, foods such as vegetables, milk (and other dairy pro-

The children pile eagerly into a scanty meal, served in the cheerless conditions of a home where the father is unemployed.

ducts), fruit and eggs were, because of their price, limited in their consumption to those with more money to spend. However, the higher prices of these goods led many farmers away from the traditional mixed farming, to specialise in dairy products, thus reducing the amount of home-produced human and animal foodstuffs still further. These shifts gave rise to the figure, quoted above, of almost a third of the British population being poorly or under-nourished, since foods which were essential to the preservation of health and strength were rationed solely by their price.

War in the 1930s and 1940s was no longer a series of battles between armies, but involved whole populations. To fight a war, even passively, away from the battlefront, required nervous and physical energy and stamina. The knowledge of what, in detail, provided such energy was now to hand, whereas it had not been 25 years before. The essential value of the so-called 'protective' foods, the more expensive ones, was realised and applied to a war situation. The principal requirement of the civilian population in a war whose effects would fall heavily on the people themselves was that their morale should not give way. Defeatism, if it arose at all, must not wear into lassitude and lack of

Tackling scrubland *below* in Norfolk meant hacking through years of growth of tangled weeds and dense untended hedgerows. The job had to be repeated over many thousands of acres.

Derelict land *above* in Essex which had lain uncultivated had to be cleared, drained and ploughed before crops could be grown on it.

will-power and energy to keep the industrial machine working. The basic requirement, then, was health- and energy-giving food. It had to be available not only to those who were accustomed to afford it, but also to those who were not.

There were 3 ways of widening the distribution of protective foods: greatly increasing production, thereby lowering the price; government intervention in the form of food subsidies and rationing; and increasing the average wage of the industrial worker so that his family budget could cope with the cost of the higher-priced foods. None of these measures could have worked on its own. In the event, a combination of all 3 resulted in the population of Britain being, in general, significantly more healthy at the end of the war than they were at the beginning.

In spite of the coming of war and the need for increased food production, the ultimate fate of the countryside was far from certain, and there was more or less constant public debate as to the place of the countryside in the list of the nation's priorities. On the one hand, there were those who saw in the revitalisation of agriculture not only a means of making Britain less dependent upon imports for her supplies of food, but also a new backbone to the British way of life. Such a broad aim was born firstly from a disenchantment with the economic ideas based on international trade and heavy industry, which had manifestly failed to increase or even maintain the living standards of the majority of Britain's people during the inter-war years. Combined with this was a more romantic, although probably no less valid, view of the value to society of the yeoman farmer and the smallholder, men and families attached to the land and the community by deep-rooted ties of husbandry and tradition.

Opposed to this vision was the idea that the country-side should be regarded primarily as a recreational area for the majority of the population who lived in the cities and manned the manufacturing industries of the nation. The extreme form of this idea, sometimes expressed, was the notion that more workers should be encouraged into the cities, since it was more economical to export in order to pay for food produced by the cheap labour of the Dominions than it was to consume food produced by the increasingly expensive labour of the British farms. The war postponed the conclusion of the debate. The long-term result remained un-decided, since no-one in the farming community was prepared to accept at face value promises about the post-war future of agriculture, after their experience in the early 1920s. The immediate result, in terms of practical assistance, was that the Government came down on the side of the agrarian reconstructionists.

In September 1939, British agriculture was far from being fully mechanised. Although more than 15,000 tractors were in operation, mainly in the eastern

War in 1939 was not confined to the Armed Forces and the youth of the country. 'Total war' meant what it said.

counties, the horse was still more widely in use as a source of power and transport. Steam-driven traction engines were also frequently seen. Machines such as combine harvesters and milking machines were used only on a few progressive farms. Many villages were not supplied with mains water or electricity. Tracts of the time, promoting the aims of rural reconstruction and revitalisation of the countryside, advocated the development of country industries based on small workshops powered by electricity specially laid on for the purpose.

Farmers who had managed to survive the hardest times of the inter-war years, by concentrating on dairy farming and avoiding the production of cereal crops, were often glad when subsidies, and later orders, were issued to plough up pasture land and begin cultivating it to the full once more. But in many places, derelict land was almost beyond reclamation. To perform some of the drainage operations to make sodden, unkempt land usable once more was beyond the means of many small farmers. Vast areas of some counties lay in this state. In Suffolk, just one example, 40,000 acres of land which once produced abundant crops lay degenerating

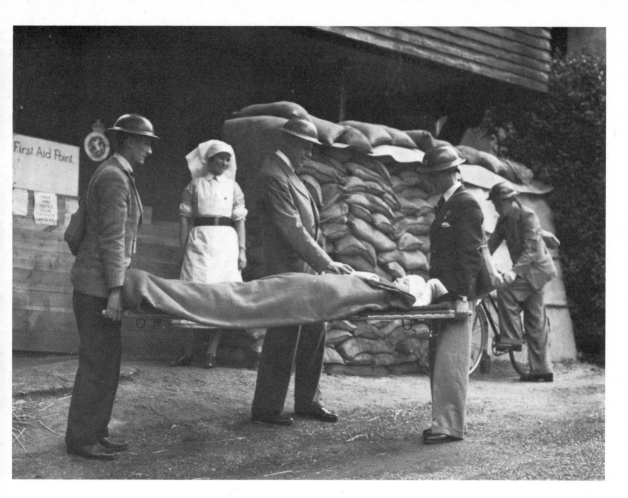

ARP exercise at a rural First Aid post.

into wilderness. The farmhouses and buildings from which it had been run were derelict, or patched together. Much of the area had been given over to the rearing of game birds, who fed well on the remnants of crops which stood unharvested in the fields. Drainage was the greatest problem in the wide areas of peaty soil in Somerset, and in the fenlands of East Anglia. In both areas, tractors and ploughs were baulked by submerged trees which had lain below the surface of the land for centuries. Frequently the Royal Engineers were called in to blast ancient logs clear of the course of new drainage ditches. In more mountainous areas of Britain, ploughland gradually covered more of the slopes than had ever been cultivated before – areas of desolate land where only sheep had been used to wander. Parts of the South Downs were cultivated again for the first time since Saxon farmers had worked the ground.

To hasten the job of ploughing, and partly to allow more light in the evenings in general, summer time was extended in 1939 until November 19th. In February 1940 the clocks were once more put forward one hour, and the nation never returned to Greenwich Mean Time throughout the rest of the war. Double summer time was introduced in 1941, making some northern areas of Britain light until midnight during late June and early July.

Agricultural preparations for war were, of necessity, slow. Far more quickly, in the summer months of 1939, the domestic paraphernalia of war began to thrust itself into houses in country areas. Most obtrusive into daily life were the preparations for the blackout. With not even the glimmer of dimmed streetlamps which occasionally shed a small patch of light in town streets, country villages became eerie, blank places, once darkness had fallen, since not a light shone from any window or doorway to give any sort of bearing. Country roads were dangerous, particularly if people walked abreast of each other, since motorcar headlights were either banned or dimmed by shields. Ditches and trees were formidable obstacles and country footpaths impossible to find. In the home, the blackout presented the problems of shuttering or sealing windows, which, particularly in older buildings, were often irregular or inaccessible in their construction. Many of the larger country houses had literally hundreds of windows to black out, which represented a tedious, time-consuming daily chore. In a large proportion of small country cottages, the only sanitation was in a hut at the end of

Love's trials *above* or a demonstration of cocktail party conversation during a gas attack. *Below* Man's best friend suffers similar indignities for the cause of freedom.

the garden and the trek to the lavatory was made even more unpleasant by having no light from kitchen door or window as a guide.

Such details loomed large in the minds of women and children who were evacuated to the countryside from the industrial cities of Britain from 1 September 1939. During nine months of 1939, the evacuees were an impending, unknown quantity to the people in the countryside, in the areas designated, because of their distance from centres of population or industry, as 'reception areas'. The possibility of the cities discharging the most vulnerable sections of their defenceless populations into the towns and villages of the countryside had taken public, official form in January 1939, when the Ministry of Health, which had overall responsibility for the scheme, asked local rural authorities to survey their areas and provide estimates of the number of evacuated children, pregnant women or invalids that could be accommodated within their boundaries. During the house-to-house survey, householders were asked to volunteer to accept evacuees. If war came, however, it was known that billeting officers would have the power of compulsion to order people to house whomsoever the billeting officer saw fit to deliver at the door. The survey had to be carried out in a complete vacuum of precedents or guidance. No-one knew accurately how many people were likely

to be involved; certainly no-one had the slightest idea of how long the evacuees would be staying in their foster-houses.

To the people in the reception areas, the whole scheme was surrounded by uncertainty. It was made no clearer by a letter sent by the Ministry of Health at the end of March 1939, informing the local authorities of the number of evacuees each would be expected to look after. The letter did not say whether the number would be made up of school-children, under-fives, pregnant women, or who, so that the authorities had little definite idea of what sort of facilities, beyond accommodation, they would be expected to provide. That they would have to provide something, however, was becoming increasingly obvious, as Hitler's occupation of part of Czechoslovakia edged Europe closer to the outbreak of war.

When the numbers of people likely to be involved became known – the scheme proposed for the whole country allowed for the movement of 3 million evacuees – doubts were raised as to the feasibility of crowding such numbers into the towns and villages of the reception areas. Providing such basic services as supplies of water and sewage systems to cater for vastly increased populations in areas whose resources were limited, even for the existing population, presented a major problem. An alternative to this strain on the

Practical in rehearsal *above*, in the summer of 1939 the horse's gas mask had yet to be put to the severe test of air-raid conditions. *Below* one of the numerous PDSA clinics for the treatment of animals injured in air raids.

China clay *above* being used to fill sandbags: air raid precautions in Cornwall, September 1939.

In the blackout *below* any steps or kerbs were a danger to shins. Municipal paintwork gave some protection.

capabilities of private homes to accept large numbers of people was the construction of camps of huts. Two months after the war had begun, however, only 6 had been built, and although another twenty-six had actually been started, progress was slow and often delayed, as workers became more urgently needed on construction of higher-priority buildings such as aircraft and munition factories. A disadvantage of the camps, from the point of view of any administrating authority, was that domestic cooking and washing arrangements had to be organised in them. Although it was never openly expressed as policy, it was obvious that private billets would have such facilities and, by force of circumstance, would simply have to share them with the evacuees whom they had taken in.

The Government did not go so far as to request that this be done free of charge. Local authorities were to have no extra burden on their rates. Individual householders were to receive a billeting allowance of 10s. 6d. a week if they were housing one child, and 8s. 6d. per week per child if they were housing more than one. This was intended to cover board and lodging, although it was hoped that communal facilities could be provided during the day to relieve the pressure on the receiving housewife. Billeted adults were expected to fend for themselves during the day, as were mothers

Bodmin hospital gets its share of the china-clay filled
sandbags – cheerful preparations for war.

and small children who were evacuated together. To
cover bed and breakfast only for these groups of people,
householders were allowed 5s. per week per adult and
3s. per child. Although the housewife was asked to
make the kitchen and other facilities available to the
evacuees during the daytime, she was under no obliga-
tion to do so and, later in the war, the sight of mothers
with young children wandering village streets, unable
to return to their lodgings until the evening, caused
much concern and no little bitterness.

During the last weeks of August 1939, the local
authorities of country towns and villages were deluged
with circulars finalising preparations and instructions
for evacuation should war break out. As Hitler made
threatening speeches concerning the fate of Danzig and
the 'Polish Corridor' of territory which he coveted for
Germany, the Ministry of Health was arranging for the
delivery of beds, blankets and mackintosh sheeting for
use in the reception areas where the evacuation had
become a far more real proposition.

Instructions arrived for the billeting of civil servants,
hospital staffs, midwives and voluntary workers, who
brought with them a billeting allowance of a guinea a
week for full board and lodging. Transference of
salary and pension arrangements for such staff had to
be effected. Lists of hospitals were drawn up indicating

how many extra beds they were expected to provide.
Instructions and advice followed on turning large
country houses into maternity homes. The requisitioning of premises was authorised under the new Emergency Powers (Defence) Act, which gave the Government enormous powers of direction over the whole
spectrum of individual, industrial and professional life.
Under its provisions, local authorities could requisition
any empty domestic premises and other sorts of
buildings, whether occupied or not, for official use in
the event of war.

Throughout the summer months of 1939, church
halls, chapels, old schools and most other similar
facilities had been offered or begged for the use of
wartime civil defence. Auxiliary Fire Stations were set
up, manned by volunteers who had come forward in
response to an extensive recruiting campaign run by
the Government. They were more or less equipped to
deal with any outbreaks of fire or bomb damage that
occurred within their area. Walls of sandbags appeared,
protecting the windows and doors of First-Aid Centres
and ARP posts, which were all scenes of ever-increasing
activity as the threat of war strengthened. Since the
Munich crisis of September 1938, during which
thirty-eight million gas masks had been distributed
throughout the nation, the ARP post had become the
centre of local wartime administration. After the distribution of gas masks and the issue of instructions for
their use, a job involving travelling long distances in

country areas, series of lectures were organised on the nature of gas attacks, the recognition of poison gas and how to deal with it if one were unprepared or without a mask. The announcement and organisation of lectures fell largely on the volunteer ARP wardens. Often they were combined with classes in more general first-aid, including emergency surgery, which provided many a lurid evening for the residents of quiet, peaceful villages.

The contrast between the outward peace of the high summer of 1939, which was one of the warmest on record, and the threat to the peace of Europe which Germany's expansion was creating was a sharp one. The pleasures of the holiday season were tinged with anxiety as wireless broadcasts and newspaper hoardings punctuated relaxing thoughts with stabs of worrying news. Many people ended their holiday sooner than they had expected. On 23 August, a non-aggression pact between Stalin and Hitler made war a virtual certainty, since, with attack from the east no longer a threat, Hitler was able to move against Poland, secure in his surmise that Britain and France, who had guaranteed Poland's frontiers, were in fact unable to back up their guarantee.

As holidaymakers left the countryside and the seaside resorts, however, their places were quickly filled. During the last week of August a number of commercial firms and institutions put their evacuation plans into operation. Many had made block bookings of entire hotels to house their staff and offices; others removed to empty country houses which had been bought, borrowed or commandeered for the purpose. Bus and railway stations were packed as people recalled from holiday by Government, firm or school, jostled with others already heading for the countryside.

On 30 August, the Ministry of Health issued a message to all local authorities in the reception areas for evacuees to have all their arrangements ready for operation at twenty-four hours' notice. At dawn on 1 September, Hitler's troops and airmen crossed the Polish border and headed for Warsaw. The Ministry of Health had issued its instruction to put the evacuation plan into operation. As Parliament debated its response to Hitler's attack, the movement of millions of women and children away from the cities had begun. On Sunday, 3 September, war was declared on the German Government. At 11.28 a.m. the air-raid sirens sounded over a wide area of southern England. Fearful, but unsurprised, many people took shelter, as the months of preparation and instruction had advised them to do. Heavy aerial attack was obviously about to begin. Evacuation had been carried out just in time.

The First World War lives again in this picture of a country town's Territorial unit setting off for their camp. The poster urging men to 'join the modern army' is more hopeful than descriptive.

New Arrivals

The transport for the prospective 3 million evacuees was organised with the precision of a well-run military exercise. The largest category, the schoolchildren, were intended to be shepherded in groups from their respective shools by teachers who would remain with them in the reception areas, attending to their education and welfare. The plan was for school groups to form up at their departure station behind barriers bearing the name of their school and the time of their train. At the sound of a whistle they would board a train and set off for their destination. In the receiving areas, they would be welcomed by local committees, given food, and then moved off in their school groups to their billets, as arranged by the local billeting officers.

Before evacuation day there were a number of dress rehearsals of these arrangements. One such took place at Hastings. The trainload of mock evacuees duly arrived from London; a first-aid post at the railway station attended to any minor accidents; and emergency rations, lent by local grocers, were distributed to 500 children within 12 minutes. Finally, communications were tested with nearby schools which were to act as distributory centres for the evacuees. With the organisers satisfied that the scheme was in running order, the children returned to London, to await the outbreak of war.

When the evacuation was ordered to begin, on 1 September 1939, many people believed that an immediate and fierce aerial attack was a virtual certainty. Uppermost in the minds of local organisers, particularly in the evacuating areas, was getting the children away as safely as possible before the bombardment began. As soon as children began to board the trains, some teachers saw the careful arrangements going awry. Schools were not being allotted specific, timed trains. As children arrived onto platforms and formed up into columns, they were marshalled onto a waiting train until it was filled, whatever the destination, so that schools who had been in touch with their intended reception area in advance were liable to find themselves in a different area altogether when they disembarked from the train. Worse still was the problem of school groups being split up because the train happened to be filled before all children of one school had boarded it. This lack of definitive destination was expected as far as evacuation from the London area was concerned, although some attempts had been made to alert the reception areas as to which age-group of evacuees, if not which particular school, they could expect to receive. Elsewhere in the country much more definite arrangements had been made, and the transport authorities' numerical logic, although efficient in removing the children from the danger areas, caused innumerable problems at their destination.

One of the causes of this disorganisation was that there were 3 authorities concerned with the planning and running of the evacuation. The Ministry of Health was nominally in overall control, the Ministry of Transport, through the various private railway and omnibus companies, covered the travel arrangements, and the Board of Education was intended to supervise the educational welfare of schoolchildren once they arrived in the reception areas. Lack of detailed communication between the 3 authorities meant that problems were passed on with the evacuees, rather than being solved. So, inadequate publicity at the outset of the scheme meant incomplete organisation at city railway stations. The removal of the evacuees from the cities being considered by the transport authorities as purely a technical exercise, involving train capacity and the numbers of people to be moved, led to a lack of co-ordination between places of departure and arrival. Local authorities, many of whom lacked the resources of staff and office space to administrate the sudden influx of people into their area, were left with the problems of numbers differing from those they expected; of the arrival of pregnant women in their area instead

The first outrage of the Second World War headlined by the *Daily Express* on the war's second day.

6 A.M. EDITION

Daily Express

WORLD'S LARGEST DAILY SALE

No. 12,258

Monday, September 4, 1939

One Penny

"We fight against evil things—brute force, bad faith, injustice, oppression and persecution—and against them I am certain that the right will prevail."—*The Premier said. Then this news . . .*

U-BOAT TORPEDOES BRITISH LINER

100 American girls were on board

LAST MESSAGE: 'SINKING QUICKLY'

1,150 passengers

A GERMAN U-BOAT TORPEDOED AND SANK THE BRITISH LINER ATHENIA—WITH 1,470 PEOPLE ON BOARD, MOST OF THEM AMERICAN AND CANADIAN—A FEW HOURS AFTER THE START OF THE WAR YESTERDAY.

A hundred American college girls—hastening home from Europe and its troubles—were among the victims of this 1939 "Lusitania" outrage.

An Admiralty report at 5 a.m. said: "The last official information we have received from the Athenia is that the ship was sinking rapidly."

The Athenia was 200 miles west of the Hebrides when she was attacked.

She was a 13,581-ton liner, built in 1923 by the Fairfield Shipbuilding Company of Glasgow and owned by the Donaldson Line.

The crew she carried was 320. On this trip she carried 1,150 passengers—many more than her normal, because of the crisis rush from this side of the Atlantic to the other.

The Lusitania was torpedoed by a U-boat in May 1915, while she was off Queenstown, with a loss of 1,198 lives.

The Athenia left Glasgow at noon on Friday, bound for Montreal. She called at Belfast and Liverpool on the way. Many of the passengers should have sailed on other lines from Continental ports, but, because of cancellations travelled to Glasgow to join the Athenia.

FLEET BEGIN THE BLOCKADE

BRITAIN'S Navy started the blockade of Germany last night. Two radiograms of one code word each put the whole Fleet on a war footing. The first proclaimed a state of tension; the second told each commander: "Begin hostilities!"

The Fleet in northern waters and in the Atlantic are concerned with our first action at sea. There are no German warships in the Mediterranean to be chased this time.

Soon after war was declared all ships using the Straits of Dover were warned that they must pass through the Downs—the eight-mile-wide roadstead between Deal and the Goodwin Sands.

Any ship disregarding this order does so at her peril. In the Downs all vessels will be examined. Those bound for Germany or carrying contraband will be stopped.

In the north waters all ships will be boarded in the open sea, what-ever the weather. Between 1914 and 1918 the twenty-two British blockade cruisers stopped 12,979 merchant steamers in the North Atlantic and missed only 642.

It is believed that some German submarines—not more than fifteen or eighteen—are already at sea. They will have to be hunted down.

From the Panama Canal zone a Dutch steamer reports that four German U-boats are fuelling at

HITLER GOES TO POLISH FRONT

BERLIN, Sunday.

HITLER left his Chancellery in Berlin this evening for the Eastern Front, where he is to assume command of the German Armies.

Four bodyguards were on the running board of his car.

In an appeal to the German Army on the Western Front earlier, Hitler said:—

"As an old soldier of the world war and as your supreme commander—I am going, with confidence in you, on the western front, to the eastern front.

"I trust that our eastern campaign can be brought to a conclusion in several weeks.

"Our plutocratic enemies will realise that they are now dealing with a different army from that of the year 1914."—British United Press and Reuter.

American Envoy bombed

From SEFTON DELMER
Daily Express Staff Reporter

WARSAW, Sunday.

MR. DREXEL BIDDLE, United States Ambassador to Poland, escaped unhurt when a German bomb dropped near his country villa this morning.

He was in his bathroom, shaving. His windows were smashed, his shaving mirror was shattered and the razor was blown out of his hand.

That is why Mr. Biddle appeared unshaven this evening when saluting cheering crowds who marched on to his embassy after calling at the British and French Embassies. Warsaw tonight is wild with joy

▶ PAGE TWO, COLUMN THREE

Theatres, cinemas closed—may reopen

All places of entertainment are closed for the present. It may be possible to reopen cinemas and theatres later.

Day schools in evacuation and neutral areas are closed for at least a week.—*See Page Seven*.

SEPTEMBER 3 SUNDAY

● AT 11 O'CLOCK yesterday morning Britain declared that a state of war existed between this country and Germany.

Notification of the state of war was handed to the German Chargé d'Affaires in London at 11 15. This constituted a formal declaration of war.

At 11.15, twenty minutes after the expiry of the time-limit laid down in the British ultimatum, von Ribbentrop invited the British Ambassador to call on him and gave him the German reply.

This was a refusal by the German Government to give any assurance about the withdrawal of troops.

The reply, it is officially stated, also included propaganda, the sole purpose of which seemed to be an attempt to lay the blame for the present war on Britain.

At 11.30 Sir Nevile Henderson demanded his passport.

● AT 5 O'CLOCK yesterday afternoon France declared that a state of war existed between France and Germany. France presented her ultimatum at midday.

(See Page Two.)

The King's message

For 15,000,000 homes

The King has consented to a copy of the message he broadcast at six o'clock last night being sent to every household in the country as a permanent record. 15,000,000 will be printed, and each will bear his signature in facsimile.

The message is on Page Seven.

Banks close today

ALL banks, including the Post Office and all other savings banks will be closed today. BUT THEY WILL BE OPEN FOR BUSINESS AS USUAL TOMORROW. There will be no money shortage.

Details on Page Eight.

Gort, V.C., will lead our troops

THE Government announced last night that Viscount Gort, V.C., will be Commander-in-Chief of the British Field Forces.

General Sir Edmund Ironside will be Chief of the Imperial General Staff, and General Sir Walter Kirke Commander-in-Chief of the Home Forces.

Fifty-three-year-old Viscount Gort will thus take over the post held by Field-Marshal Lord Haig in the war of 1914-1918.

General Gort was appointed Chief of the Imperial General Staff in December 1937 at fifty-one, the youngest man ever to hold the post.

The War Minister (Mr. Hore-Belisha) said: "This is a soldier of genius," and cut red tape to

▶ PAGE TWO, COLUMN FIVE

WINSTON BACK

He is First Lord; Eden is the new Dominions Secretary

By GUY EDEN
Daily Express Political Correspondent

ONE of the first acts of the Prime Minister, as soon as Britain's declaration of war became effective yesterday, was to reconstitute the Government and to set up a War Cabinet of nine Ministers.

Mr. Winston Churchill enters the cabinet as First Lord of the Admiralty—the post he held in 1914—and Lord Hankey, former chief of the Cabinet Secretariat, becomes a Minister without Portfolio. Both have seats in the War Cabinet.

Mr. Anthony Eden becomes Dominions Secretary, without a seat in the War Cabinet, but in order that he may be in the best position to maintain contact between the War Cabinet and the Dominions he will have special access to it.

The War Cabinet will be the supreme executive body responsible for the conduct of every aspect of the war. The members, whose average age is sixty-one, are:—

PRIME MINISTER.
Mr. Neville Chamberlain.
CHANCELLOR OF THE EXCHEQUER.
Sir John Simon.
FOREIGN SECRETARY.
Lord Halifax.
MINISTER FOR CO-ORDINATION OF DEFENCE.
Lord Chatfield.
FIRST LORD OF THE ADMIRALTY
Mr. Winston Churchill.
WAR MINISTER.
Mr. Hore-Belisha.
AIR MINISTER.
Sir Kingsley Wood.
LORD PRIVY SEAL.
Sir Samuel Hoare.
MINISTER WITHOUT PORTFOLIO.
Lord Hankey.

Lord Stanhope, former First Lord of the Admiralty, becomes Lord President of the Council, and Sir Thomas Inskip, former Dominions Secretary, becomes Lord Chancellor.

Sir John Anderson, former Lord Privy Seal, becomes Home Secretary and Minister of Home Security. He will continue to be in charge of A.R.P.

It was announced last night that Sir Archibald Sinclair, leader of the Liberal Opposition, had declined an offer by the Prime Minister of a post in the Cabinet, on the ground that in present circumstances the Liberals could give better service to the nation and the Government by supporting all necessary war measures from an independent position

---

Crowded with children a train prepares to leave Paddington station for a destination in Wales. ARP notices underline the grim reason for their journey.

of teenage children, or vice versa; of part of a school party arriving, whilst the rest of its number might have been deposited fifty miles away – a problem which frequently taxed the Board of Education. None of the national authorities gave leadership strong enough to organise concerted action, so problems were often solved piecemeal, in an improvised way, to the detriment of the smooth running of the scheme as a whole.

The difficulties of evacuation were compounded, ironically, by the fact that people did not either register or turn up on the day for evacuation in as great a number as had been expected or intended. This problem was most noticeable in London, where the largest number of people were involved. As it became clear what was happening, on the first day of evacuation, the second day's programme was brought forward to fill out the first. Schools which had been instructed to leave London on the third day of evacuation were hastily reorganised into leaving on the second. Although the press hailed the improvised arrangements as a triumph of quick thinking and efficiency in the face of imminent danger (as, in one sense, they were, since the children were removed from the likely bomb target areas quicker than had been intended), they meant that

any plans which had been made between evacuating and reception areas had to be completely abandoned.

A typical example was that of a secondary school from north London. The boys were divided into groups of ten, care having been taken that brothers or friends were in the same group as far as possible. Each group was in the care of one adult, who had notes on the habits and characteristics of each boy in his group. The boys travelled by one train to the outskirts of London then changed trains for the next leg of the journey. At the end of their rail journey, they were loaded into a number of buses. At each change, the carefully constructed group system suffered, as the boys were continually organised by the police into crocodiles of different shapes and sizes. The destruction of the system came when the buses took the boys to a number of different destinations. To complete the scattering, in some of the villages the boys were collected from the local reception centres and billeted before any register could be made of their names and the school they belonged to. Almost two weeks passed before all the boys were located once more.

Once the mass movement was over (and, to the credit of the railway and bus companies, it was carried out without serious physical casualty), the problems of the *ad hoc* nature of the organisation of the reception areas began to multiply. Since probably no more than 2 million of the 3 million expected evacuees actually

The reception area *above* The WVS refresh the evacuee children before they set out on the final stage of their journey to their foster-homes. *Right* Announcement of the Southern Railway evacuation service, issued on 31 August.

moved to the countryside, there was a certain amount of room for manoeuvre and some reorganisation of billets was undertaken in order to bring school parties closer together. There were also a number of complaints, from the guests who had volunteered to be moved into the countryside and from the hosts who, in the last resort, were compelled to put them up, which could only be solved by changing billets. The local billeting officer came under pressure from both sides and often had a most thankless job to perform.

The Ministry of Health was concerned that the billeting officer should be a local man, well acquainted with his area and the people in it. In practice, this had possible disadvantages. In some places, the billeting officer was a local tradesman and, having some desire not to offend his best customers, avoided billeting evacuees on families who could well afford the space and any expense it might involve. In others, a poor billeting officer might use his powers to make life more difficult for richer families whom he happened to dislike. The alternative to a local billeting officer, however, was someone completely strange to the area, appointed by a distant bureaucratic authority, which might have had worse consequences still. The fault lay in the fact that the system contained no provision for adequate and frequent consultation between the central and local authorities, so that peace and fair dealing in the billets depended on the strength of character and tact of the billeting officer and the success of his improvised decisions.

In the event, evacuees who remained dissatisfied simply went back to the cities. From the first day the flow of women and children brought up in the streets of cities who found life in the country intolerable, even for twenty-four hours, was a steady one. For many, the lack of department stores, cinemas and fish and chip shops was not compensated for by the abundance of fresh vegetables (which were strange to some city palates), rabbits and eggs. Country hosts were shocked by the lack of common table manners, shown by many of the city children, who were accustomed to eat a slice of bread and margarine wherever they happened to find themselves, and their disregard for washing habits considered to be essential to health by their hosts. Their guests saw no pleasure in living conditions where water had to be fetched from a well, oil-lamps provided the only source of light, and the only sanitation was an earth-closet some yards from the house itself. The 'phoney war', the non-arrival of the devastating bombing which the evacuation scheme had been devised in order to avoid, made it easier still for many evacuees to think of returning home. To many wives away from home, a husband left fending for himself in a cold house was a hard thought to bear. To parents left in the cities, the absence of their children filled them with as many anxieties as the threat of bombing. By the end of the first month of the evacuation scheme, half of the mothers and a quarter of the children had returned to the cities.

The lack of clear direction from the Ministry of Health allowed a number of problems to become serious bones of contention between guest and host. Not the least of these was the payment the host was to receive for the upkeep of evacuee children. The basic payment of 10s. 6d. per week for the first child and 8s. 6d. for any subsequent children was supposed to cover food only. Clothing was to be provided by the child's parents. Areas in between these obvious categories – items such as laundry, soap, medicine, shoe repair and so on – were often argued over, and could only be resolved by recourse to the billeting officer, whose only useful source of aid was his own initiative and tact.

There were innumerable instances in which the arrangements worked well and the two families established a friendly and sometimes lasting relationship. But there were times when the difference in circumstances created a gulf which was difficult to overcome. Evacuees from very poor families arrived in old, scruffy clothes with no others to change into if

The first meeting between host and evacuee guest. The billeting officer prepares to take her leave, her duty discharged.

their things were wet. Many country mothers were surprised to find that pyjamas were often thought useless and unnecessary by poorer city families. The difference between the two ways of life was on many occasions diminished by the hosts reclothing the children they had taken in, if only for the reason that they felt ashamed that shabbily-dressed children should be seen walking in and out of their houses.

Sometimes city parents felt that differences in living standards and habits ought not to be diminished; that their children were being taught ways and manners which would estrange them from their own families. Different manners created problems of

Evacuees, arriving at their reception area, dejectedly await the organisation of their billets. In some areas children had to wait for many hours before being taken in.

discipline for the hosts – they could find themselves in the quandary of having either to let a visiting child behave as it would at home and then appear to the family, and probably to itself, odd and out of place, or else to try to persuade it to conform to the customs of the family it had entered, which might prove equally difficult. Some children were unable to settle down with children already in the family, or else country children might resent the intrusion of strangers whom their parents sometimes made over-obvious efforts to love and to treat as part of the family.

Probably the worst problem that the hosts had to face was the number of lice-infested children among the evacuees. In households proverbially spick and span, such infestation was regarded with the utmost horror and considered by many to be beyond the pale of what they ought to be asked to put up with. In some areas of the country, almost half the evacuated children had lice breeding in their hair, and the WVS and other voluntary bodies were called in to assist in a major disinfecting campaign. In a Scottish town, the medical officer bought up a consignment of hair-clippers and shaved the heads of an entire trainload of infested mothers and children evacuated from Glasgow.

Second only to lice was the problem of bed-wetting. It was not surprising that so many children wet their beds, since they had been uprooted from their homes following some more or less unimaginable threat of destruction from the air, had travelled, in uncomfortable conditions and without their parents, to an unknown destination, to be greeted by people they did not know and who claimed to be going to look after them for some unspecified period of time. For children of all ages, the journey and the new circumstances must have been very upsetting. To the housewives who had taken them in, the problem was far more physical then psychological, consisting of a mound of unwanted laundry. For months, nothing was done to relieve the problem, although some wise communities found that understanding care and attention for the disturbed children overcame all but the most serious cases. Eventually, hostels were opened for chronic bed-wetters, and a supplementary laundry allowance of 3s. 6d. a week was made payable to any housewife who still sheltered a bed-wetting child. On the whole, however, problems with children, or those who actually remained in the country for some months, were gradually overcome and many evacuee children retained fond memories of the families who had given them shelter in their flight from the cities.

Far more intractable were the difficulties which arose when a child accompanied by its mother was

billeted on a family. The intrusion into the privacy of each housewife was much greater and conflicts over domestic arrangements, particularly in the kitchen, inevitably occurred. The financial arrangements for billeting a mother and child made the situation even more fraught. An evacuee mother was expected to provide her own meals during the day, either using her hostess' kitchen, which could not be made a compulsory facility, or by fending for herself in whatever cafés or restaurants the local village or town had to offer. In some areas in the heart of the countryside such resources were hard to come by, and billeting house-wives found themselves forced to share their kitchens. Various solutions were tried, one of the most common being a shift system, in which the billeted mother and child were asked to cook and eat their meals after the family of the house had had theirs. In other house-holds the evacuees were asked to eat their meals in their bedroom. The results were rarely satisfactory for either party.

For most mothers who had sent their children away, the time spent apart was filled with wondering how the children were faring and feeling anxious about their happiness. The railway companies organised cheap excursions for mothers to vist their children and many

Evacuees being taught to plough by a Devon farmer.

took advantage of them, if only to spend a Sunday with the children. To enter the house of a strange woman who had taken her place as a mother, if only temporarily, was rarely an easy thing to do and the situation was eased only by great tact and sense on both sides. Some hosts refused to offer hospitality to visiting mothers, considering that they had done their duty in looking after their children, and left them to their own devices, often on a Sunday afternoon when cafés or teashops, if there were any at all, were very likely to be closed. Other visiting mothers abused their own position, treating the journey to see their children as a chance to gain a free tea for relatives who came along for the ride as well as themselves.

In general, as far as the people of the reception areas were concerned, the worst of the problems of the Government-sponsored evacuation scheme were over by Christmas 1939. Insoluble difficulties had been dissipated to a large extent by the numbers of people who had decided that life in the countryside, whatever the circumstances in the cities, was just not for them. Those who remained were either borne with a good grace or found themselves in a situation which was actively enjoyed on all sides. Of these last there were not a few.

Strange features *above* of life in the countryside for city children: domestic wells and outdoor sanitation were novelties whose attractions soon wore thin for many evacuated city-dwellers.

Behind bars *below* evacuees wait for the train which will bring their mothers to the country for a visit to their foster-homes.

Children were affected by the war in a variety of indirect ways. *Above* The British Empire, celebrated here by west country children on Empire Day, 1940, was still an ideal which many people believed in and were fighting the war to preserve. *Above left* diminutive evacuees find comfort in an elaborate pram, their cares transferred to the anxious lady who looks after them. *Left* more grown up, the children from a WVS-run nursery have graduated to a donkey-cart. *Below left* special billets and hostels were

organised for the under-5s, or children who had suffered from the emotional upset of evacuation. *Below centre* evacuation camp made up of concrete huts, for families bombed out of Portsmouth, Hampshire. *Below right* a group of boys organised into collecting salvage. *Right* the loner, who prefers to collect old bones his own way. *Above right* the village cobbler sets a group of evacuees to learning a useful trade during their stay in the countryside.

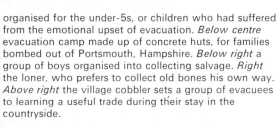

The BBC evacuated many of its staff to Bristol. Here *Garrison Theatre*, a popular wireless programme, is produced in a makeshift studio in a converted church hall.

At the time there was much criticism in the press and in parliament, particularly during the first two months of the war when nervous tension, keyed up by the expectation of a terrible bombardment, had to be released. Any measures which could be criticised were. The organisation of the scheme was described by one set of commentators as displaying all the marks of having been devised by middle-class men with no conception of the needs or wishes of mothers and children, particularly of the poorer city dwellers, whose sorry conditions of living were revealed to many shocked eyes for the first time. If nothing else, the state evacuation scheme disclosed areas of degrading poverty and need which gave a solid impetus to some of the measures of social reform which, through force of circumstance and individual effort, were brought about during and after the war.

As well as bearing the burden of the state's evacuation of private individuals, many country towns had to find space for the influx of businesses, government departments, hospitals or private schools which had had to make their own arrangements for escape from the danger areas. For the smaller private schools, this often entailed more than one upheaval, as a number had

removed from the cities to the coastal areas of Sussex and Kent. When the aerial activity over this part of the country became intense during the summer of 1940, earning for it the nickname of 'bomb alley', the schools were forced to move again, inland and farther west. Although the phoney war period had persuaded a number of evacuated institutions to move back to London, accommodation in the safer areas was hard to find, and many schools had to struggle on, sharing inadequate premises.

The areas they left behind, the coastal towns of Hampshire, Sussex, Kent, Essex and Suffolk, suffered a gradual decline in their population, which accelerated after the fall of France in June 1940. With the invasion of Britain suddenly a real possibility, few people wanted to remain in the way of what would be the obvious route for a German invading army and air force. After the example of the panic-stricken refugees in France, harrassed by dive-bombing Stuka bombers and clogging the roads, hindering the defending forces, the Government advised people to leave the area as quickly as they could. More than 330,000 people left the south-eastern coastal areas during the summer of 1940. In Folkestone, which was not only an obvious landing point for a German invasion, but was also within range of shell-fire from the German guns on the French coast, the population dropped from 46,000 to 6,000. Many shops put up their shutters for months;

Internees a group of German nationals being escorted along a quiet street into Douglas, Isle of Man.

High Streets were deserted except for military traffic; grass grew in the cracks in the pavement.

Further west, the story was the exact opposite. In Torquay, for example, large hotels were emptied of tourists as sizeable city companies such as the Prudential Assurance moved in most of their staff and equipment. Country houses were popular evacuation centres for many firms and institutions. Bankers set themselves up in a mansion near Stoke-on-Trent; the National Union of Teachers took over a manor house in Gloucestershire; the National Association of Local Government Officers had to be content with a holiday camp in Croyde Bay, north Devon. One of the most extensive institutional evacuations was undertaken by the BBC, which moved many of its London staff out to its regional stations. Near Evesham in Worcestershire, a large mansion was converted into studios and offices. Conditions in the town, where actors, actresses, announcers and technical staff were billeted, were far less regal and some of the older local residents, who considered anything remotely connected with the stage undoubtedly immoral, imposed their own restrictions on the leisure hours of their guests. But the BBC staff at Evesham were probably far more fortunate

than those evacuated to the supposedly safe areas of Bristol and Manchester, where, when the blitz came, conditions were no different from those in London from which they had escaped.

They at least were able to move on again. For one group of people moved out of the cities into the countryside, there was no such freedom. Throughout the 1930s, refugees from Germany and Austria had entered Britain. Mostly Jewish, the numbers of refugees arriving increased dramatically in the winter of 1938 and continued unabated through 1939 as the Nazi party carried out brutal pogroms on the Jewish population. Many of the refugees intended to re-emigrate to the United States, Canada or Australia. A number took up work permits and settled in Britain; some were able to set up businesses and created jobs which were filled by British employees.

On the outbreak of war, all known foreign nationals from countries which were now enemies of Britain were required to appear before tribunals to show good cause why they should not be interned, lest their national sympathies should prove dangerous to the British war effort. More than 74,000 men and women were examined by these tribunals and they were classified into 3 groups. The first, known as Class A, admitted to or were strongly suspected of being pro-Nazi: these were interned immediately. Class B, their classification based largely on their recent arrival in Britain, were subjected to restrictions on their movements. By far the majority, at least 64,000 people, were placed in Class C and allowed the liberties of any British citizen.

They remained free to go about their business until 12 May 1940. The war in Europe had reached a new pitch of violence. Holland and Belgium were losing the battle for their survival against the Nazi forces; at home, Chamberlain's Government had fallen and Churchill was in the process of forming a new administration. With the threat of the German armies approaching ever closer to the Channel, the British civil authorities looked to the defence of their shores, villages and towns with hasty trepidation. A surge of fear followed rumours of traitorous activity on the Continent and the ease with which German forces were overcoming resistance which was believed to be riddled with enemy agents. Overnight a belt of land stretching the length of the British coast from Inverness southwards and westwards to Dorset was declared a 'protected area'. Within it all male Germans and Austrians between the ages of sixteen and sixty, whatever their examined category, length of residence in Britain or occupation, were rounded up and despatched to improvised internment camps. The protected area was a wide belt of land and included such towns as Cambridge. Distinguished academics, senior members of the staff of the London School of

Economics, which had been evacuated from London a few months before, were suddenly removed from their work. The internment was supposed to be temporary, but its net was indiscriminate and secretive and the police who carried out the arrests were able to give no clue as to how long the victims' detention was going to last. Unlucky 'enemy aliens' who happened to be visiting friends or relatives by the seaside were taken away at a few hours' notice.

Four days later, on the 16 May, all male members of Class B enemy aliens between sixteen and sixty, wherever they lived, were taken from their homes with the minimum of warning. The peremptory knocking on the front door in the middle of the night, the fear of which haunted so many of the refugees before they had fled their homes, had caught up with them at last in Britain, the haven of democracy and civil liberty.

Internment gained momentum and encompassed both men and women. The invasion of the north-west of Europe by the Germans, the clandestine operations of Scotland Yard against the enemy aliens and lurid publicity in favour of internment in some newspapers fostered a wave of sentiment against all foreigners and against Germans and Austrians in particular. When Italy entered the war on the side of the Nazis, on 10 June, attacks on Italians and Italian property broke out in many towns. By then the protected areas had been extended farther along the coasts and farther inland. All foreigners, 'enemy' or 'friendly', except the French, were subjected to a curfew from 10.30 p.m. (midnight within the London boundaries) to 6 o'clock the next morning. Special permits were needed for any 'friendly' foreigners to remain in a protected area.

By mid-July, about 20,000 Germans and Austrians had been suddenly detained. Regardless of the reasons for their being in Britain, Nazis and anti-Nazis, Jews and Jew-baiters were herded together in one operation and imprisoned behind the same barbed wire. One of the earliest internment centres was the exhibition hall at Olympia in west London. In perpetual semi-darkness, since blackouts covered all the windows, with bare benches and boards for seats and beds, the first internees began their imprisonment. Along with prominent Nazis who had been in England on the outbreak of war, men who were intimate friends of Hitler or senior officers in the Gestapo, leading Jewish figures were gathered in. One such was the former Vice-President of the Berlin police, who had been one of the men most wanted by the Nazi régime after he had fled the country. Many others were refugees from Austria and Czechoslovakia who had escaped from the Nazis. Being interned together, with the slogans of Nazism ringing through the barren hall of Olympia, was a bitter experience for passionate anti-Nazis who were desperate to fight against all that the Third Reich stood for.

Internees behind the barbed wire which isolated the group of hotels at Douglas, Isle of Man, which formed one of the largest internee camps in the British Isles.

After a few days in the gloom of Olympia the first internees were taken by train to Clacton in Essex. On arrival, they were marched through the streets to Butlin's holiday camp which had been requisitioned for use as a prison camp. One of the Jewish internees noted the reactions of the people who watched them march through the streets. Some taunted the internees scornfully; others looked on them with sympathy as the first victims of the war; a noticeable number raised their arms in the Nazi salute and prophesied their quick release by an approaching Nazi régime in Britain.

Butlin's at Clacton was the height of luxury as far as

internees were concened. Even so, the prisoners had to walk from the chalets in which they slept to the dining hall across wet, muddy ground, and were only allowed to do so under armed escort. The chalets themselves were made less agreeable when barbed wire was attached to their roofs, which made them leak. When it rained the prisoners were forced to suffer sodden beds and flooded floors since their only other shelter was the dining hall, unreachable except at mealtimes. Dampness and hunger pervaded another holiday camp turned over for the imprisonment of internees at Seaton, in Devon. It was situated below sea-level, with flimsy huts for sleeping in, riddled with draughts. Prisoners arriving had to sleep on bare timber boards, without blankets.

On the outskirts of Bury, Lancashire, a derelict cotton factory was used as a transit camp. It was in-fested with rats, the floors were rotten and the windows broken. The only light came from the broken glass roof, which let in the rain as well. The 2,500 internees were guarded by armed guards who patrolled the perimeter of the building between two barricades of barbed wire. Inside the factory there were eighteen water-taps which were supposed to serve as washing facilities for the entire camp population. There was one bath-tub. Sixty buckets served as lavatories. Medicine was issued by the camp commandant, but only on payment. Although the only accommodation was the rooms in which the internees slept, some men, eminent in their academic fields, managed to organise classes and lectures in the afternoons, to pass the time and to keep up spirits.

The movement of prisoners from camp to camp was unceasing. One group of prisoners underwent a typical

A group of tractors *above* engaged on ploughing up land which had lain uncultivated for decades. *Left* advertisers had to come to grips with the fact of shortages and still try to make their products appealing to the public.

journey from the transit camp at Kempton Park racecourse in Surrey to the Isle of Man. The journey was estimated to take seventeen hours. For the journey each man received a large piece of bread, and each group of fifty men a lump of cheese. A soldiers' bayonet had to be borrowed to cut up the cheese since the prisoners had no knives or sharp instruments. When the cheese had been divided there was a portion about an inch square for each man. Eight hundred men were packed aboard the ship from Liverpool to the Isle of Man. Since soldiers barred the way to the saloons, the men had to stand on deck for 2 hours. It rained during the entire journey and continued to rain as the men stood for a further hour on the dockside at Port Douglas on the Isle of Man. They marched for an hour in the rain to their camp, where there was no food to be had that night, only tea.

The general trend of internees' journeys was always in the direction of Liverpool where prisoners waited for transport to the Isle of Man or across the sea to Canada. On the Isle of Man hotels and large seafront houses were commandeered and ringed with barbed wire to form permanent prisoner-of-war and internee camps. The interned refugees were subjected

Steam power from a ploughing engine which had seen service in the First World War, drags a plough and its crew across a field.

to conditions in the camps to which they were taken which, because of their temporary nature, were often far below the standard of military prisoner-of-war camps. Protests about their accommodation by internees and requests for their release were rarely satisfied quickly since there was no neutral protecting Power or international convention which governed the running of internee camps as was the case with their military equivalents.

The gradual emergence of the facts about internment prompted a fierce public reaction. The muddled and panic-stricken way in which internment had been carried out was as severely criticised as the questionable principles of interning and deporting men who were only suspected, and that through no other reason than the fact of their nationality, of harbouring thoughts inimical to the British cause in the war against the Nazis.

As many internees, British residents for many years, or sympathetic to Britain's stance in the war, struggled with the wartime bureaucracy in order to obtain their release, the farmers in the countryside around them were crying out for extra men to help them work the newly-ploughed land which the Government had urged

them to cultivate. During the first months of the war, plans were brought into operation retaining agricultural workers on farms rather than calling them up into the Forces. Farm work was made a reserved occupation for men over twenty-one years of age, and for those between eighteen and twenty-one who were considered indispensable, for reasons of their particular skills or lack of any other man to do the job. The rebirth of the Women's Land Army, which had seen service in the fields during the late years of the First World War, provided a pool of enthusiastic if inexperienced girls whose conditions of service were that they should be prepared to be sent anywhere and do any agricultural task that they were asked to carry out.

During the first winter of the war, however, the services of the WLA were seriously under-used. The winter was a hard one, one of the coldest in living memory. Heavy snow in January followed by hard frosts in February meant that ploughing was delayed until March. When farmers were at last able to harness their teams of horses or hitch a plough to their tractors, they found that they could either manage the ploughing with the same number of farm workers they had employed the previous year, or that there were men available locally, either unemployed or who worked on a casual basis, to make up the number needed.

Events abroad and in Westminster during the late spring of 1940 significantly affected the farmers' situation. The German advance across Europe brought home to the British Government the true nature of the Nazi preparedness for European war and the obvious threat it posed to the very life of Britain as a free nation. Belatedly, thoughts were turned to the increased production of arms, munitions and particularly aircraft, as the type of the Nazis' warfare became clear. To the people of the countryside, this meant two things. Industrial wages began to rise at an increasing rate as the urgency of the situation became apparent. The need for labour to man the factories grew and the attraction of the higher wages diminished the numbers of agricultural workers. New building made an impact on rural land; not only were new ordnance factories built for obvious reasons in areas which would not at first sight attract enemy fire, but new military camps for the vastly increased Forces, and new airfields for the RAF were hastily constructed.

In May 1940, the Germans reached the coastline of north-west Europe. Neville Chamberlain resigned and Winston Churchill took his place as Prime Minister of Great Britain. The vigour with which Churchill began to pursue his task and the renewed determination which his oratory instilled into the heart of the British people were reflected in the activities of the Ministry of Agriculture. The new Minister, Robert Hudson, supervised the conclusion of a minimum wage agreement which set the lowest level of agricultural wages at £2 8s. per week. Although this was far below what could be earned through working long hours of overtime in the heavy industries and in the munitions factories, it brought the farm workers' wages up to a level not significantly below the wages which could be earned in any other industry. At the same time, the Ministry of Labour prohibited employers from taking on workers who had previously been engaged in farm work, and agreed to direct all unemployed men with agricultural experience back into farm work.

The farmers themselves requested an increase in the minimum wholesale price of the goods they produced, in order to cover the costs of increased minimum wages and the extra labour they would need to cope with the new Government's food production targets. In reply, the Government adopted the principle of paying the farmers not only an increased price based on the cost of production, but a price which included an element of extra profit, intended for the farmer literally to plough back into his land, in order to increase production further the following year. Although the fixing of the wholesale price of individual commodities caused some problems, since the price level was one means by which the Government could encourage increases or decreases in the production of each commodity, the guaranteed income (discounting factors outside governmental control, such as the weather) which, it was promised, would be maintained for at least a year after the war

was over, encouraged the agricultural community to make the huge extra efforts necessary to increase production to the level demanded of it.

The detailed governmental administration of farming was carried out through the local War Agricultural Executive Committee, which came to be known as the War Ags. During the autumn and winter of 1939–40 the committees had given guidance, which was generally well received, and material assistance through the loan of machinery to enable farmers to cope with the extra ploughing which formed the foundation of the programme for increased crop production. Hudson strengthened the War Agricultural Committees by the introduction of staff from the county Farm Institutes as technical and scientific advisers. He enlivened his own communication with the local situations by appointing a number of men distinguished in the agricultural world as liaison officers.

With the administrative framework thus strengthened, the War Agricultural Committees were

The Women's Land Army a hostel near Slough receives a visit from the Duchess of Kent.

ordered to make a quick but detailed survey of each farm, to assess its productive potential and decide whether it were at present fully equipped or efficiently managed to fulfill that potential. With the stronger administration went a sterner brief, for the Committees were instructed by the Minister to deal firmly, to the extent of eviction if necessary, with farmers who, through incompetence or neglect, were not making the best of their land. Poor farmers had little enough excuse for failure. Increases in prices had given them a firmer financial base. The War Agricultural Committees were authorised to supply seeds, fertilisers or lime, on deferred terms if necessary. In some instances, the Committee, by agreement with the farmer, farmed the land themselves, again for a payment which could be deferred. Its final power was the requisitioning of some or all of a farmer's land, which would be farmed under the auspices of the War Agricultural Committee, or let to an approved tenant.

Such sweeping powers were obviously open to abuse. During the war years almost 770,000 acres of land were requisitioned. Within this total, nearly 1,400 farms in England and Wales were requisitioned

which farmers and their families had to leave. One of the harshest features of this rigorous policy was that there was no means of appeal against the War Agricultural Committee's decision. And some decisions were punitive indeed. A farmer of Marlborough, Wiltshire, had farmed his land for twenty-eight years when in 1940 the Wiltshire War Agricultural Committee ordered him to plough fifty acres of his grassland in order to grow oats. Since there was no labour available the Committee took responsibility for the job. It was done badly and the acreage yielded only half the potential crop. The same thing happened the next year. The farmer's appeals for extra labour went unanswered and although the Land Commissioner for the area inspected the farm and approved of the way it was run, the farmer was given five weeks' notice to leave the premises. His appeal, heard by the Committee who were evicting him, was turned down and the farmer was removed from his home simply because he was unable to carry out the Committee's orders.

In Warwickshire a farmer and his family were turned off their farm, which was taken over by a member of the War Agricultural Committee who lived

nearby. Although he did not need the farmhouse, the family were turned out. Since accommodation was so scarce the father and his younger son were forced to live in a disused hen-roost, where the man's elder son found them when he returned on leave from the Army.

The problem of lack of help on the farm was suffered by an elderly man in Northumberland, whose only worker, his son, had been called up. The man, aged sixty-seven, was struggling and the War Agricultural Committee ordered him to give up the farm. In despair, since he had nowhere else to go, he shot himself.

The old man's suicide was a tragedy, but the case of a farmer from Hampshire reveals just how far civil authority extended over the lives of British citizens in wartime. The farmer had been born on his farm, which his father had owned and farmed before him. On 17 April 1940, the farmer was ordered by the War Agricultural Committee to plough up one of his fields in order to grow crops. The farmer, believing he knew his land better than the Hampshire Committee, refused to do so. He was immediately given notice to leave, which he rejected. On 22 July, the War Agricultural Committee ordered his eviction. The farmer desperately bolted his doors against the police, armed himself with his shotgun and retreated to the upper floor of his farmhouse. Teargas failed to remove him. After an exchange of shots, the police broke in to the house. The farmer continued to resist arrest and was shot dead.

The only body with any authority to challenge the Committee's decision was the Ministry of Agriculture, but the War Agricultural Committee was a powerful executive branch of that same body. The situation was not adjusted until the Agriculture Act of 1947.

Occasions such as these, when the War Agricultural Committee came into such violent dispute with a tenant-farmer or owner-occupier, were extremely rare. More often the co-operation between them produced valuable increases in the productivity of the land. The survey of land undertaken by the War Agricultural Committees in 1940 showed that much of the extra land otherwise available for cultivation was so badly drained that it was waterlogged. The work of repair and renewal was a major job. The obstructions to progress in this direction during the 1930s, caused by the confusing patchwork nature of the powers of local water authorities, were swept aside by the immediate

The WLA at work *above, left* in a WLA hostel, curtains painted on the wall add a homely touch to spartan surroundings. *Above centre* and *right* instruction and training, in a converted railway carriage, and grouped around a tractor. *Middle left* a team of foresters swings through sylvan glades. *Bottom left* charcoal burning, an ancient trade, being carried on at Leckwith, near Cardiff, in the spring of 1944. *Left* WLA girls pump poison gas into hedgerows to clear them of rats.

necessities of war. With new machinery supplied by the War Agricultural Committees, rivers were dredged and new banks built up; streams were cleared of obstructions, widened and deepened; new ditches and drains were laid in the fields themselves.

This supply of machinery was one of the most obvious benefits the organisation of the War Agricultural Committees conferred on British wartime farming. During the first months of the war, a contract with the Ford Motor Company provided a certain number of tractors and cultivating tools. The main source of supply, once Lend-Lease agreements (under which Britain imported goods and machinery in return for sharing her military facilities abroad) came into force between Britain and the United States, was from the agricultural machinery manufacturers in America. From the spring of 1941 large numbers of heavy tractors were imported for earth-moving and land reclamation projects. Other implements such as disc-harrows, to break up more acreage of grassland, binders and combine harvesters, for the harvesting of the planned increase in cereal crops, and many smaller items were also imported in increasing quantities.

The war-aim of Churchill's Government was victory, nothing less; and the people, it seemed, shared his view. From May 1940, the nation was wound up to this end. The numbers of men and women gathered into the Forces increased; those who were left behind were sucked into the industrial machine supplying them. In this way the pool of $1\frac{3}{4}$ million unemployed men,

WLA girls set off for a day's work in the fields from their permanent but mobile homes.

which was a legacy from the depressed economic times of the 1930s, was soaked up, leaving few men available to fill the force of 100,000 workers estimated by the Minister of Agriculture to be needed to fulfill the new food production targets. Of those who were available, not many had agricultural experience. There were three other main sources of labour: the prisoners of war, who might or might not fall into British hands; the conscientious objectors, who refused to serve in the Forces; and the volunteers of the Women's Land Army.

From the spring of 1941, the WLA had little difficulty in finding places for the girls who had volunteered to join. By 1943, more than 80,000 WLA girls were working on the land. The problems that the organisation of the Land Army threw up were totally new to farming. On the one hand, the girls were in the main volunteers from the town, with no knowledge of farming techniques, practices or skills. The work had to be simplified and closely directed. Yet at the same time the girls were often employed in groups larger than normal on British farms, if they were engaged on reclamation or drainage schemes. The close, informal relationship between a farmer and his small groups of assistants, whom he might have known for a number of years, did not hold with the new Land Girls. Some, of course, developed in this way, if one girl remained on a particular farm for some time. Often, the Land Girls filled a vacancy for a season, or travelled about from farm to farm as the need arose. Consequently accommodation was a major problem. Single girls could usually be found a place to sleep in the farmhouse or a neighbouring cottage. For groups of girls working in teams, special hostels were needed, all of which took

The foreman of a WLA ploughing team attempts to free a plough which has become snagged on a buried root – a common occurrence when ploughing previously uncultivated or derelict land.

administration and extra staff to look after them.

More difficult still was the search for enough fore-men to oversee the work, to explain the details of the job, and to assume responsibility for the immediate and local solutions of problems of job or domestic organisa-tion. One of a foreman's most difficult tasks was to find a variety of jobs for a team of girls, should weather conditions change whilst they were on a particular task, or the time of year mean that a succession of smaller jobs had to be done in between land reclamation, drainage, ploughing, planting and harvesting.

To many people, the WLA was the least glamorous of the women's war services. The uniform was unat-tractive, and the Land Girls' function outwardly unassuming. The tremendous amount of hard work they carried out, often in very uncomfortable conditions, was sometimes forgotten. Yet by the standards of today, the conditions of the Land Girls' service were

stern. Land Girls were contracted to work a 48-hour week in winter, and a 50-hour week in summer. They were paid a minimum wage of 22s. 6d. per week, after board and lodging had been paid for. If a girl were between seventeen and eighteen years, her wage was only 18s. She was entitled to a minimum of 6 working days' paid holiday a year, plus the usual public holidays. After every 6 months of satisfactory service, any girl working more than twenty miles from her home was provided with a free return rail warrant so that she could visit her home. Apart from these regulations, and her entitlement to sick pay, the Land Girl's conditions of work were in the hands of the farmer or the War Agricultural Committee who employed her. She had safeguards, in that the WLA's county organisation included representatives who visited the Land Girls and their accommodation to ensure that conditions were up to the minimum standards. But the range of jobs she could be asked to do was limitless, and the outdoor conditions under which she might have to do them were beyond anyone's control.

The most frequent task the Land Girls performed

A convoy of Army lorries *above* towing 6-inch howitzers passes through the village of Bossington in Somerset. The denuded signpost bears only a question mark.

Uprooted signposts *right* take on an unfamiliar duty as obstacles to enemy aricraft which might try to land.

was assisting with, or looking after, the milking of a dairy herd, and all the cleaning, feeding, bottling and washing jobs which went with running a small dairy. Otherwise she was engaged on general farm work – jobs without end – which included ploughing the fields, weeding and hoeing them, spreading on dung to manure them. Later in the year there would be the lifting of potatoes and other root crops. Hedges needed attention and renewal, ditches had to be kept clear and firmly banked for good drainage of the land. During the vital few weeks of the late summer, the Land Girls on farms were at the heart of the tasks of haymaking and harvesting and threshing the cereal crops. With the drive for increased production unable to guarantee a longer period of fine weather at the beginning of the autumn, more crops had to be harvested in the same few weeks as before.

Other Land Girls were directed into more specialised agricultural tasks, on fruit farms, or in private or commercial market gardens. Equally specialised were those girls who operated the heavy machinery of the earth-moving gangs, or the dredges maintaining the rivers and their banks. Yet others took up the lonely tasks of forestry, jobs which involved walking many miles through often difficult woodland, selecting trees for felling, and doing the job themselves, or measuring timber, picking out trees to be used as telegraph poles, replanting woods and forests with new trees and many other tasks. Yet others became ratcatchers, or thatchers of hayricks. Almost all the jobs were previously foreign to women's experience. The overriding claims of war destroyed most of the barriers of tradition or prejudice both on the part of those who already worked on the land or those who volunteered to do so.

During the summer of 1940, war appeared in more tangible form all over the countryside. Strangers to any country area were given no clue as to their whereabouts after 31 May, when all signposts were ordered to be removed, village nameboards taken down and shopsigns with the name of the locality on them painted out, to avoid giving any geographical assistance to an invading enemy. Buses reworded their destination boards with the names of local landmarks or pubs rather than towns or villages. Complete mystification of an enemy was very difficult, since local names were often carved into

milestones or the stones of churches or graveyards, but the attempt was made, as many milestones were buried where they were, never to be dug up again.

One of the most feared German weapons was their force of airborne troops, who had played an important role in German attacks, particularly on Belgium. Although parachutists could not be stopped from landing, fields, parks and all accessible open spaces were littered with an assortment of obstacles to prevent aircraft from touching down. These ranged from custom-built erections of iron poles to old farm carts, disused cars, drainpipes and any other objects which could possibly serve. A similar assortment was found blocking many country roads, as roadblocks were set up at strategic points on the outskirts of towns or villages. Many of these were more permanent, made of iron posts sunk into concrete bollards. Others would have been little hindrance to an invading army: trees trundled across roads and lashed to a post on either side were intended primarily as nuisance value in the event of an invasion. Such roadblocks were frequently manned or overseen by Britain's largest single wartime body of men, who were formed to harry the enemy should they land, or to assist the local authorities in the maintenance of order and local defence. The butt of numerous jokes, they were the male complement to the Women's Land Army as the least glamorous and possibly most underrated of Britain's defending forces – the Home Guard.

The Prime Minister and two staff officers inspecting a village barricade, manned by gunslinging 10-year-olds prepared to fire at anything or anyone.

More Expected

Crops ripened well in the superb summer of 1940, which was even better than the long days of sunshine of 1939. Haymaking went ahead much as normal. Farmers in most areas of the country seemed set fair for achieving the high production targets set by the Government for food for human and livestock consumption. If the weather held, and the harvesting was not delayed for lack of men to gather the crops, all, it seemed, would be well. All, that is, except for one unanswerable question which nagged at everyone's mind: for whom would the crops be harvested?

By the end of June the Germans were masters of the northern coastline of Europe. From the French and Belgian airfields the German air force, the *Luftwaffe*, were only minutes away from the counties of south-eastern England, barely an hour from London, and within range of all England, Wales and almost all of Scotland. That they would shortly invade Britain was highly probable. No-one doubted that if they did so they would come in large numbers by air as well as by sea. In 1940 the use of parachute troops was part of the new method of warfare being waged by the Germans. Although they had in fact been used principally in surprise attacks on nations technically at peace with Germany, such as Holland and Belgium, their prowess and their numbers were matters for awesome rumours in Britain. How the parachutists would fare against defenders who had declared war on their Government, who expected them and who promised themselves to fight to the last ditch was an untried question. Their reputation, certainly, ran high.

Churchill, in one of his earliest acts as Prime Minister, wrote to President Roosevelt of the United States on 15 May 1940 that he expected Britain to be attacked from the air by bombs and parachute troops, in the very near future. The public in general had no means of telling what limits there were to the German

Coastal battery with its crew leaping to action stations during a defensive exercise.

September 1940 Posed but disturbing, this picture catches something of the defiant, devil-may-care mood of the summer of 1940, when Britain stood alone against the triumphant Nazis.

air fleet, how far they could travel, and where they would choose to attack. From fields throughout Britain, farmers and their workers looked into the sky and imagined the pattern of low-droning planes and the silent flights of deadly parachutists swinging slowly down through the air, intent on reducing their land to a food production unit of the bloated German Reich.

In London, guards were posted outside the BBC and the governmental departments. BBC news broadcasts carried warnings for everyone to be on watch for an attack by parachutists. Anthony Eden, the Secretary of State for War, broadcast an appeal for able-bodied men to join the Local Defence Volunteers. The press called the LDV the 'Parashots'. No-one else did, but the significance of the name was plain. Throughout the country men and women were on the alert against attack. The threat from the sky served to seal the bonds of unity created by Churchill's speeches in the face of the military catastrophe on the Continent.

Another anxiety sometimes threatened to divide people from each other, particularly in small, isolated communities. Fifth Columnists were seen, or suspected, in the most unlikely guises. Fifth Columnists were as recent a phenomenon as fearsome parachutists. The

name, describing a group of people working on behalf of an external enemy inside a citadel or nation in order to bring about its downfall, originated in 1936 during the Spanish Civil War. The imagined threat provoked the British Parliament to pass a far-reaching Treachery Bill, on 22 May 1940, which provided for the death penalty to be used against anyone giving, or appearing to give, any sort of assistance or information to the enemy's forces, or preventing the defenders from carrying out their tasks. The official seriousness with which the activities of an as yet unidentified Fifth Column were treated was given weight by the pronouncement of General Ironside, the Commander-in Chief of the Home Forces, when he spoke to LDV commanders on 5 June 1940. He told them to beware not only of suspicious-looking characters, but also to look closely at the 'best-behaved and the most sleek' as being equally likely to be up to no good.

The social background of divisions in British society which had made themselves plain during the 1930s provided fertile ground for implanted suspicions to regenerate and multiply. The political nature of the industrial divisions between the owners of the industries and the workforce; the rise of the Communist party and a social fashion for adherence to its tenets; the establishment of the British Fascists Organisation; all provided ready-made sources of fanatical dissension which could easily be developed into suspicions of

The Prime Minister inspecting coastal defences in the north-east of England, his finger with relish on the trigger of a tommy-gun.

. . . meanwhile, in Britain, the entire population, faced by the threat of invasion, has ...ng into a state of complete panic . . ."

national treachery on either side. The numbers of refugees who had entered Britain both before and during the first months of the war provided a convenient if spurious umbrella for the imagined entry of the large body of spies and saboteurs who were presumed to make up the Nazi Fifth Column in Britain. Most of the refugees had arrived in a hurry and in large groups, making it impossible to ensure that every one was genuine.

Disguise was an important factor in what was discovered, after the war, to be the myth of the Fifth Column. In May the Dutch Foreign Minister had told a press conference in London that German paratroops had descended on his country disguised as nuns, Red

A blockhouse disguised as part of a seaside roundabout on a promenade in the north of England. The forlorn horse and the scattering of rusty barbed wire emphasise the grimness of the wartime scene.

The coastal community was affected by the war in a direct way. *Below* invasion notices made sombre reading at Lowestoft.

Cross nurses, monks and tramcar conductors. The idea took firm root in the public mind and many inoffensive brothers and sisters of the church were subjected to a disconcertingly searching scrutiny as they were passed in the street. At its worst, the Fifth Column scare was a useful excuse for paying off old scores, and the police received numerous anonymous letters containing information advising them to pay attention to a local dignitary who might at some point in his or her life have incurred the letter-writer's displeasure.

In spite of the obvious ludicrousness of companies of nuns swinging from parachutes, rifles concealed in their voluminous habits, the complementary notions of airborne attack and secretive treachery were important in the decision to ask the men of Britain who were not already in the Forces to volunteer to form local units of a nation-wide defending force. The appeal was broadcast on the wireless on 14 May 1940, by Anthony Eden. It was directed at men between the ages of seventeen and sixty-five. All who were capable of 'free movement' were invited to enrol at their local police stations.

The response was vast, and temporarily overwhelmed smaller police stations who ran out of enrol-

An armed train on the Romney, Hythe and Dymchurch Light Railway sets off to patrol a stretch of the south-eastern tip of England. Its usual load of holidaymakers has been replaced by Lewis guns and Boys anti-tank guns.

ment forms. Within twenty-four hours, a quarter of a million men had enrolled. The first immediate problem was the organisation of the new force. It had been brought into being extremely quickly, since the German invasion of France had made the defence of Britain itself of prime importance, and most of the Regular Army was bottled up in Flanders. At first the Government relied on local men, preferably ex-officers too old to serve in the Army. The Lords-Lieutenant of each county were asked to appoint a senior officer from amongst the volunteers, who would then choose his immediate subordinates, who would in turn choose men to organise the LDV into local battalions, companies, platoons and sections.

In most areas of the country, particularly in the cities, this took some time, through the sheer size of the administration, which had to exist at first on volunteered time, money and facilities such as premises and secretarial equipment. In the countryside, where areas of local command were more easily defined, some LDV units were organised much more quickly. On the coastline of Kent and Sussex, where the danger of invasion threatened most obviously, patrols were on watch before the first day of recruitment was over.

A number of the first officers were men who had served as such in the First World War. For many it was an agreeably nostalgic experience to be 'back in harness' once again, however much the LDV differed from the discipline and organisation of the Regular Army of 1914–18. Of course the LDV had had no time to develop any traditions or customs of its own. To many of the younger recruits the ways of the First World War were not for them. The LDV began its life with an air of democracy and organisation by common consent which was never present in the Regular Army. Ranks at first were kept to an absolute minimum. Many platoons were formed as a result of meetings in village pubs or private front rooms, in which positions of responsibility were decided on by means of a vote. One recorded example of the resentment attracted by the nostalgic play-acting of some First World War officers occurred in a small village in Devon, where one man who applied to join the local LDV company was told that he was not of the correct social standing for that particular unit, which was composed of a retired army captain and his colleagues of twenty-two years before. Elsewhere generals served alongside butchers' boys as privates in the LDV.

In the battalions of the countryside – and it was largely for the defence of the countryside that the LDV was formed – there was often a decidedly sporty note. Members of local hunts were highly valued as volunteers for their knowledge of the surrounding countryside. Platoons which were formed to defend the wide expanses of open ground owned by golf clubs were popular ones to join and membership of them was open to a very select few. The most important areas the LDV had to cover were the millions of acres of virtually undefended agricultural land, which, in the convinced belief of the time, was highly vulnerable to attack from the air.

The first duty of the LDV was to wait, watch and report anything suspicious either to the Army or to the local police. In some areas the police were not immediately co-operative with the LDV, regarding them as an amateur and ill-defined body of men with unspecific duties and powers which might make them more of a hindrance than a help in time of emergency. In most places the new force, being composed of well-known local faces anyway, settled into its developing routine.

Regular observation posts were set up, in some spot which commanded a good view of the town or village or surrounding fields. Church towers were very popular. The clear, warm nights of the summer of 1940, spent watching the stars and waiting for the dawn to come up over low, golden hills produced many a romantic memory of the first few months of the LDV. Shepherds' huts, converted caravans, mills, castle towers were all pressed into the service of the network of eyes waiting to trap any stranger, whether he had descended from the sky or not. There were, of course, innumerable false alarms, so that slowly-moving animals, a peculiar-shaped tree, courting couples or late-night strollers were frequently challenged, to the embarrassment,

often to the mild amusement of all those concerned.

Less amused were the police officers, particularly those of higher rank, whom the LDV challenged on the grounds that they might be spies or Fifth Columnists masquerading as guardians of the law. The LDV was one of the bodies authorised to ask anyone to produce his or her identity card, part of the private citizen's statutory paraphernalia of war, on pain of arrest if the card were not produced. Not infrequently the police would react with a counter-charge, creating a situation which usually dissolved through its absurdity.

Anti-Fifth Columnist activity also involved the setting up and manning of road blocks, which were supposed as well to hinder the movement of German troops, should the landing take place. At first the road blocks were primitive affairs – oil drums filled with rubble spanned by a tree trunk or strands of wire. Some consisted merely of a piquet formed by overturned farm carts or other equally flimsy obstacles. The streets of Margate were barricaded with bathing machines, filled with sand.

Throughout the war, the only person truly inconvenienced by these roadblocks was the ordinary motorist, whose life was quickly made purgatorial by the enthusiasm with which the LDV held up traffic. Since supplies of petrol gradually dwindled and more and more cars were laid up this became less of a hazard as the war went on. But hazard it certainly was,

The ancient market hall provides the meeting place for these Local Defence Volunteers of a Midland village, cheerfully preparing to face the foe.

Local Defence Volunteers, *above* one in uniform, the other with simply a field cap to show his status, hold their rifles shot-gun fashion.

A well-armed band of Exmoor farmers *below* on patrol in the early days of the LDV.

as the LDV took its duties more and more seriously. When small arms became available, anyone ignoring the LDV's requests to halt was liable to be shot without further ado. To be informed, as a number of women were, that one's husband had been shot dead by an amateur band of lookouts, most of whom had only the haziest notion of how to use a weapon and who were little better organised than the local darts team, must have been one of the harshest experiences of the war.

The organisation and the status of the LDV were put on a much more solid footing during July and August 1940. The name of the force was changed, on the suggestion of the Prime Minister, to the Home Guard. The battalions were given county titles, to correspond with their counterparts of the Regular Army. By November 1940, military ranks and the insignia to go with them had been introduced. To many members of the Home Guard who were ex-servicemen this was a satisfying procedure, clarifying relationships and laying down guidelines for organisation. The Home Guard assumed an official presence at the War Office and the full panoply of services ancillary to an armed force – secretariat, stores, official transport and all the regulations and paperwork that went with it – attached itself to the Home Guard.

To a number of the younger recruits this was not such a happy sign. It gave full scope to those who were

"*I grant you it* MIGHT *be a bit awkward if the invasion came up Cherry Lane instead of the High Street.*"

prone to live for the sake of a military establishment and whose retirement had been impoverished for the lack of it. It meant that officers and non-commissioned officers were part of a descending chain of command rather than, as had often been the case, the elected leaders of a group of men who had banded together to protect their village. The Home Guard became more military, more rule-bound, eventually better equipped and better clothed. But the days in which it had established itself as a small piece of English folklore were over.

Before the upgrading of the organisation had fully worked its way through the force, however, the Home Guard had to face a situation in which many of its members in the south and east of England thought that the final test of their courage and fighting skill had come. On Saturday, 7 September 1940, after weeks of heavy fighting between the RAF and the *Luftwaffe* in the skies over south-eastern England, Hitler ordered the first major raid on London. During the late afternoon 300 bombers and 600 fighters flew in a huge formation over the Kent coast and followed the Thames estuary towards the London docks. The Chiefs of Staff of the British Forces were meeting in Whitehall to discuss the

Emett's cartoon *left* was made poignant as well as funny by the fact that the situation he depicted was so near the truth in many places. *Below* Special constables man a flimsy roadblock in a country lane.

Home Guard in the home: a farmhouse kitchen turned into an armoury. Guns are cleaned while the pastry is being made.

imminence of invasion. The sight and sound of the bombers unloading their cargoes over the East End of London left them in no doubt: the invasion was about to begin.

The nation's defences had to be in the highest state of readiness. The Royal Navy was already prepared to sail at a moment's notice to reinforce the Channel patrols. The RAF was on constant watch and put up a defence against any and every hostile aircraft which crossed the sea from Europe. The Army units were ready to move at 8 hours' notice. The Chiefs of Staff decided that this was too long. The one further step which could be taken to wind the defensive spring as tightly as it would go was to issue to the Home Forces a codeword previously agreed to mean that conditions were ripe for invasion; that troops should take up battle stations; and that certain telephone and telegraph lines were to be appropriated for military use only. The word was *Cromwell*.

The codeword was issued from London to eastern and southern commands of the Home Forces, and to the other regions for information, at 8 o'clock on the Saturday evening. From the outset it caused immense confusion. Few officers who received the message seemed to be aware of its true meaning. Most knew that it bore grave implications concerning invasion, and assumed that Germans were actually landing on British beaches. Many communications officers in other regions of Britain failed to grasp that they were being sent the message for information only, and troops were ordered to battle stations as far north as Scotland. While these troops far out of the firing line were awaiting the attack, some units in the south and east were not at full alert, since, for some reason, the message did not reach some coastal units until midnight.

The Home Guard had got wind of it, however. Church bells, silent for some months, since the ringing of them had been designated as the signal that the invasion had begun, pealed across the countryside, rousing sleeping Home Guards, air-raid wardens, police and any one else to whom the bells meant that the end was nigh. The roadblocks, reinforced since the early days, swung into position, hindering rescue services from the home counties from getting to the London docks which were ablaze and under constant attack from fleets of German bombers. Non-official callers were turned away by telephone operators. Bridges near coastlines were demolished by Royal Engineers. Throughout the night the defenders along the beaches, on the hilltops, in the church towers and manning the roadblocks gripped their weapons and strained their eyes into the darkness, ready for the first glimpse of the German invader.

Neither on that night, nor on any other night during the war, did an invading force of German soldiers set foot on British soil. But the alert had proved one thing: that the Home Guard were on their mettle and prepared to stand to their defences if any emergency arose again. The alert continued for almost a fortnight. Then restrictions on movement, particularly of service personnel, were gradually relaxed. By the third week in September the crisis had passed. Invasion became less likely as autumn approached. The conjunction of fair weather with tides favourable to the invading force was unlikely to occur again in 1940.

Even had it done so, the Germans had abandoned the plan for the invasion of Britain, and had set their course for Moscow. This fact, of course, was unknown to the British people in 1940 and the Home Guard, having passed through its first period of extreme crisis, in some places with a shade of regret that it had not been able to prove its valour, prepared to make itself more efficient in the use of what weapons and other equipment it possessed.

The Home Guard's armour was the subject of the earliest jibes about its inadequacy to defend the country and its inhabitants against any sort of organised attacking force. Although Eden's broadcast calling for volunteers had promised that the new force would be uniformed and armed, the number of volunteers, and the fact that no organisation existed to marshal and supply them, meant that military clothing and, to many volunteers far more important, guns were in very short supply. In the earliest days, whatever came to hand was eagerly seized upon. Ancient firearms were discovered in dusty cupboards; sporting rifles and shotguns were highly prized; museums and galleries were scoured for serviceable guns, however old; theatres gave up rifles and pistols which for years had been used only on the stage. Even these exertions produced only a small proportion of the number of weapons needed to supply the rapidly-growing force. Many men were armed simply with some form of a cosh, whether newly-made, improvised out of pieces of lead piping or wooden staves, or merely some household article commandeered, such as a hammer or a chair-leg. One unit was advised to arm itself with cudgels or heavy walking sticks. It was a vain hope that such implements would do much harm to armoured and motorised divisions of the German army. Nevertheless men had them in their hands and could grip them firmly with a resolve that was many times more satisfying than simply sitting at home beneath the threat of invasion wondering when it was going to come.

Slowly, more deadly weapons began to filter through to the Home Guard platoons. As the force was

so widespread and so numerous, no one man could call a rifle issued to him his own, since two or three often had to be shared amongst ten or a dozen men. Some of the first to arrive were American Springfield rifles which had been embalmed in heavy grease since the end of the First World War and needed hours of strenuous cleaning to make them serviceable once more. The British rifle of the First World War, the Lee-Enfield, was far more popular and a modern version was available in limited numbers to the Home Guard by the end of 1940.

Automatic weapons were more highly regarded still, and it was a phlegmatic Home Guard platoon which did not relish the thought of the day when their first machine-gun arrived. Lewis guns, Browning Automatic Rifles, Vickers water-cooled machine-guns and Thompson sub-machine guns, familiar throughout the film-going world as the American gangsters' standard weapon, all filtered through to the Home Guard who gained much in self-confidence and morale when such powerful armour came into their possession.

It was one thing to sit behind such a weapon and visualise a Nazi soldier in line with the gunsights. It was another matter altogether to instil into amateur soldiers the knowledge and practical expertise to be able to maintain the weapons and operate them quickly and correctly under conditions of active warfare. A combination of the invasion scare in September

Vital training *above left* a Home Guard platoon studies its first Vickers machine-gun. *Above* practice on the rifle range watched by amused colleagues. *Right* anti-aircraft practice, with wooden models and stout string providing the target.

and the shortening of the days as winter approached, which meant the temporary cessation in country areas of the all-night watch for invaders, strengthened the enthusiasm for thorough weapons training. In conjunction with any local military camps and with the aid of ex-servicemen in the ranks of the Home Guard, evening or weekend training courses were arranged which selected members of each company or platoon would attend. They would return to their own platoons and, in a barn or village hall, outhouse or private room, wherever the platoon's headquarters were situated, would retail the information to their fellow men.

Lectures and classes on the theory of machine-gun assembly and operation or the uses and techniques of hand grenades occupied many a winter evening. Often they were supplemented by army training films. Sometimes more useful instructions came from veterans of the Spanish Civil War, versed in the techniques of guerrilla warfare. From Finland came the device known as the Molotov cocktail – a bottle filled with any inflammable liquid, with a petrol-soaked rag for a fuse stuffed into its neck. Molotov cocktails were effective when they worked, but were also chancy things to have on one's own side of the battle lines, since any unlucky spark could set them off.

Gradually the Home Guard accumulated a whole armoury of bombs and grenades, most designed for uses against tanks. With them came a variety of grenade and missile launchers, since tossing the bombs by hand often posed as much of a threat to the defenders as it would to an advancing enemy. A barrage of flames was another popular notion for defence against a motorised enemy. It was thought particularly suitable for narrow country lanes, with high banks on either side, which could form a lethal trap when flooded with petrol and ignited. Many such flame traps were created in the lanes of southern England by means of a device known as a Flame Fougasse. An oil drum was filled with a mixture of tar, lime and petrol and buried on its side in the bank of the lane. At the appropriate moment a detonator ignited the mixture which burst out of the drum and stuck in a flaming mass on any object which happened to lie in its path. Aligned in groups of four they were highly effective, and simple and fairly safe to operate.

Correct use of all these weapons had to be based on continuous training and practice, and this was often

Strong point on the edge of a wood, manned by members of the Home Guard undergoing a training programme in defence of the countryside.

the most arduous task that many of the Home Guard who had never soldiered before had to face. Where arms were concerned, particularly rifles, ex-servicemen could carry out the drill attendant on bearing them correctly and efficiently with the precision that had been drummed into them as long as twenty-five years before. Many civilians, particularly farmers and game-keepers, were handy with a shotgun and could fire a rifle perfectly well. But, for the sake of discipline in action, a body of armed men serving as an official defending force had to be disciplined 'in camp' and on parade.

Many of the Home Guard had never shouldered arms in their life and found the crisp, apparently simple, movements of the parade ground more intricate than they had expected. The first training sessions were often held out of the public eye. It was bad enough being regaled with shouts of 'Thank God we've got a navy' as they went out on patrol un-uniformed and obviously under-equipped, without laying themselves open to ribald comments on their first attempts to master the art of bearing arms in the military fashion. In a way the Home Guard were particularly sensitive to comments and criticism. They were a volunteer force so their predicament was of their own making. They were also a local force, so that everyone who saw them had quite probably known them all for many years. The time they gave to the

Home Guard was their own time, outside their working hours, and since it could amount to twenty or thirty hours a week or more, time spent away from home learning an apparently superfluous rifle drill was often resented, particularly by wives, who were less inclined to be seduced by the romance, of which there was an undoubted element, of 'playing soldiers' with real guns.

In no department of their activities were the Home Guard more sensitive than on the question of their uniforms. At first there was no uniform, the only distinguishing feature of a Local Defence Volunteers being an armband, known as a brassard, with the letters 'LDV' stencilled on to it. The first proper uniforms to be issued were the equivalent of the overalls used by the Regular Army for fatigues – loose-fitting jackets and trousers made of coarse denim cloth. Field-service caps were also promised, but it was a rare Home Guard company that was issued with both caps and uniforms. It seemed axiomatic that whatever was issued was either much too large or so small as to constrict all movement. Since there were not enough uniforms to go round, those that were available had to be shared, making it impossible to carry out any permanent alterations. By the autumn of 1940 the

denims were being replaced by serge, army-style battledress, which, apart from the usual problems of fit, was much more popular. Being so, it brought with it greater problems when a platoon was issued with too few sets of the uniform, since those who turned up regularly to parades and training sessions generally considered that they had first claim on the new uniforms. The battledress often had to be rounded up from the homes of the regulars who were loth to part with it for the sake of sharing its use.

Many ex-officers already had uniforms, and it was a serious source of contention as to whether they should be allowed to wear them or not. Most members of the Home Guard agreed that it was obviously bad for morale if some were forced to appear in public in ill-fitting denim fatigue-suits, whilst another member of the same platoon, ostensibly of the same Home Guard rank, appeared resplendant in his general's uniform, complete with decorations from previous campaigns. The problem pointed up the difference in attitude which lay beneath the surface of the apparently democratic nature of the early Home Guard. Some members felt that officers who flaunted the uniforms of their service careers were more interested in establishing the codes of social division which were prevalent amongst army officers, than in developing the desperately-needed efficiency of the Home Guard as a fighting force.

Water-bound patrol of the Home Guard, armed with a Lewis gun and an American rifle, both of First World War vintage.

Invasion exercise in which 'paratroopers' are discovered infiltrating the defences in a hay wain.

In wearing their old regimental uniforms, such men were disobeying orders, and although, at first, no-one could be compelled to join the Home Guard, those who did were required to comply with instructions from those responsible for the organisation and running of the force. The pride which most members took in their organisation, however shamefacedly in its early days, and which was essential to its efficient operation, was insulted by men who did not conform to its co-operative ethic for the sake of reliving the social vanities of their previous military careers. Inevitably such ex-officers, if they were placed in charge of a body of Home Guards, did not get as much joint effort from them as did one who was prepared to put up with the same conditions and annoyances as every other man. The regulations concerning the uniform were emphasised early in 1942, when the War Office, under whose auspices the Home Guard was now organised, issued a specific order that only the regulation uniform, issued by the War Office, should be worn. Privately-tailored uniforms, of whatever style or age, were expressly forbidden.

The Directorate of the Home Guard, a special department at the War Office, surprised civilians and ex-servicemen alike with its uninhibited administration of the volunteer force. The Home Guard had come into being too quickly for a rigid bureaucratic machine to be set up to run it. The Directorate was aware too, that it was dealing not with a body of men who were paid professionals, under orders to do a job of work, but with unpaid volunteers who were giving up their free time in order to assist in the defence of their country. Such men needed different treatment if their enthusiasm were not to be diminished through frustration by administrative procedures. The Directorate also shielded the Home Guard from a certain amount of criticism from senior professional officers who felt that it was a debasement of their calling to allow that part-time amateurs could be trained to do anything useful to aid the Regular Army in the defence of Britain. They were joined in their view by members of the German High Command, who did all they could through wireless propaganda to pour derision on the strength, skill and fitness of the Home Guard.

Through 1941 the Home Guard's organisation increased in strength. The appointment of officers, which in the first *ad hoc* organisation of the force had devolved from the Lord-Lieutenant of each county largely through the military and social class structure, was taken over by a Selection Board, detailed specifically to ignore 'political, business or social affiliations' in its examination of potential officers. At the end of the year the Government included the Home Guard in its provisions for military conscription. From January 1942, any male civilian between eighteen and twenty-five could be directed to attend at his local Home Guard patrol for up to forty-eight hours a month, for training

The 10th Hertfordshire Home Guard *above* engaged in a street fighting exercise.

Ludlow Castle *below* once more in arms, manned by a garrison of the Gloucestershire Regiment.

or guard duties. A number of men resigned, as they were entitled to do, being volunteers, considering that the nature of the force had changed, that the danger of invasion was decreasing, or that they could no longer commit themselves to a specific number of hours of duty. If they did resign, they faced the possibility of being conscripted back in again, from which there was no resignation.

The stricter organisation had its compensations. The supply of weapons and uniforms improved and training programmes had instilled into most members of the force the basic practices of observation, sentry duty and the maintenance and use of weapons. With the introduction of a defined number of hours' attendance each month, duty rosters were easier to draw up, although at some periods of the farming year the introduction of compulsory attendance caused some difficulties. Many men involved in running a dairy herd who were at work for 10 or more hours, 7 days a week, could hardly be expected to attend a regular weekly parade. Harvest times and haymaking were particularly busy times of year when Home Guard company commanders, many of them farmers themselves, had to forget the rule book and attend to agricultural tasks which could not wait. This was particularly true of weekend exercises, during which men would be given permission to leave their posts to attend to milking, after which they would return to their military duty. Such arrangements became an important part of the exercise itself, since even if an invasion occurred,

A rick-thatcher gets on with his job while the Army swarms around on field exercises.

milking would have to go on. In spite of the difficulties of combining rural and military tasks, duties were being carried out with a degree of skill that surprised the Home Guard themselves. The force numbered more than a million and a half men, adequately supplied with weapons to carry out its appointed tasks.

As the Home Guard exercised and manoeuvred, more ambitious roles than simply observing and reporting or manning road blocks were conceived for it. Until the end of 1942, the emphasis had been on static defence – manning the roadblocks and overlooking gun emplacements, from which the Home Guard were expected to defend the lanes and villages to the death, fighting to the last man to stem the enemy's advance. More movement was prescribed in the exercises for 1943, in which Home Guard units could break away from their static positions and form a mobile defence force if the situation demanded it. This notion was extended, some thought to absurd lengths, the following year. 1944 was the year of D-Day, the Allied landings on the coast of Europe, when the whole of the south and south-east of England was packed tight with British, American and Commonwealth troops waiting to embark upon the invasion of Europe. Some commanders thought that in an attempt to hinder the great operation, the Germans might counter-attack by dropping parachute troops into southern England.

Farmyard exercises for the Army involving a Bren-gun carrier, a mortar, ladders, wagons, much hay and busy personnel. The farmer keeps an eye out for the safety of his poultry from the sanctuary of his hut.

With the regular troops occupied with launching the invasion, these enemy paratroops were to be the responsibility of the Home Guard. More mobile reserve units were created, with orders to roam the fields flushing out the invaders and dealing with them appropriately.

Such attacks never came, and as the Allied forces slowly pressed the German armies back towards Germany, it was obvious that the Home Guard was never going to have the dubious pleasure of meeting its adversary face to face. A number of its members felt that this was a sad thing, that they had been cheated out of their 'show'. Many more considered that they

had done their duty, that they had been on hand when they were needed, and spent many hours, often in extremely uncomfortable conditions, prepared to fight until they were felled, for the sake of their small patch of ground. It was enough, and if the final test had not materialised, so much the better.

From September 1944, direction of men into Home Guard service ceased, and attendance at parades became voluntary once more. Enthusiasm began to wane but the numbers of men engaged on Home Guard activities had hardly diminished when the final order for the force to 'Stand Down' came on 1 November. Many felt that this was rather a sudden and peremptory end to their activities. The habits of more than four years' service, for those who had volunteered after Eden's broadcast in May 1940, were hard

to break. Most of the Home Guard officers were engaged in rounding up arms, ammunition and other equipment to return to the military authority which had issued it. For the private soldier his term of duty was over. There was a national Stand Down parade in Hyde Park on 3 December 1944, and similar local parades up and down the country. For the men of the rural areas, it was a matter of being able to concentrate wholeheartedly once more on the business of farming, without the interruption of drill or guard duty or Sunday parades or watching through the night for an enemy to drop from the sky.

For a tiny minority of Home Guards, action against enemy soldiers became something more than a matter of constant training and a vivid imagination. In the areas of the country which housed German

'**Divine Discontent**' leads 'Deadeye Dick' through quiet lanes on a sunny afternoon in a southern English village.

prisoners of war, the Home Guard were always on the alert. If an incident occurred they took few chances. One such took place near Grizedale Hall, in the Lake District. The Hall, a POW camp for captured German officers, was converted for its purpose from an empty, dignified, if bleakly situated, country mansion. For a brief period before the war it had been a holiday camp, peopled, presumably, by holidaymakers wishing to get far away from the hurly-burly of life. The nearest shops, in the village of Hawkshead, were 3 miles away. In between lay bare moorland, wild in the summer, completely desolate in winter. Some miles away to the west lay Coniston Water; to the east, Lake Windermere. Possible escape routes lay only to the north or south of these lakes, across very barren country. Yet some men tried. One U-boat commander was forced to, by the strict ethics of his fellow-officers, who decreed that because he had surrendered his submarine on its maiden voyage, to a Hudson aircraft, he was not to be tolerated at the camp. He was given to understand that if he did not attempt to escape, he would be summarily dealt with by his fellow officers.

The man, Leutnant Bernhard Berndt, took his chance and made his attempt. He escaped from the camp and managed to remain hidden throughout the night. In the morning he was found 2 miles from Grizedale Hall, sheltering beneath a tarpaulin in a farmyard, by two members of the Home Guard. Challenged, he gave himself up, on the assumption that since he had managed to escape from Grizedale he would be sent instead to another camp. Instead, Berndt discovered to his horror that his captors were taking him straight back to Grizedale. Suddenly he fled, hopelessly, across the field. The Home Guards fired warning shots, but he did not stop. They fired again and Berndt fell. Within a few minutes he was dead.

Berndt was a naval officer. Most of the Germans who landed on British soil were airmen who had been shot down in battle. When arrested, if not by the military or by the Home Guard, German prisoners were handed over to the Army, firstly for interrogation by officers from their equivalent service, then for internment until the war was over in one of the many camps dotted about the country, usually in sites chosen for their inaccessibility and the lack of cover for an escaped prisoner that might be found in the towns. Frequently, country houses proved ideal accommodation. Normally the supervisory staff lived in the main house and the prisoners in converted outhouses or huts built for the purpose. Surrounded immediately by barbed wire, and then by quiet, unpopulated grounds, the prisoners were afforded little chance of escape.

For the first years of the war, few German prisoners attempted to. Many, particularly from the *Luftwaffe*, were so sure that the German invasion of Britain would

Italian prisoners-of-war setting off for work in local fields in the summer of 1941.

come soon and overwhelmingly successfully, that there was no need for escape. They could sit back, secure in the knowledge that release was virtually at hand. As the years passed and news reached the prisoners that the attacking German armies had turned their backs permanently on Britain, more men tried to get away. Few managed to travel far. Of those who reached the coast of Britain, none crossed the sea, either to Ireland or to the Continent. With no underground movement to help them on their way, to the Germans, Britain was a prison island.

As the war developed and Allied victories began to occur, the trickle of prisoners arriving in Britain increased, and the total eventually went into hundreds of thousands. A large proportion were Italians, captured at sea or in African campaigns. From the camps in the countryside for non-commissioned officers and other ranks, many parties of prisoners were sent out to help with agricultural work. Their clothes were distinctive, having large green patches sewn on to their dark blue overalls. As far as the Italians were concerned, it was found hardly necessary to provide them with distinctive clothing, since few ever attempted to escape. Sometimes they worked in the fields in groups of up to thirty or forty and would be overseen perhaps by only one British soldier, who, in

the fields on a hot summer's day, was rarely at the peak of his concentration. The Italians were generally liked by the people of the countryside and the farmers who employed them. Many, coming from farming communities, were only too pleased to get back to the land.

Although German prisoners who worked in the fields or on the roads were far less popular, being in general of a more sullen, less carefree disposition than the Italians, it was acknowledged that the work they did was efficient and highly productive. Many were employed on the heavier land-reclamation schemes of draining and dredging.

Prisoner-of-war labour in the fields of Britain was mainly a sight of the middle and later years of the war. In the autumn of 1940 there were as yet few enemy prisoners in British hands; many fewer than the Germans had taken in their sweep across Europe. In most areas of the country, October and November closed in with the prospect of even harder work to come, ploughing up more grassland for new sowing of cereal crops, potatoes and beet. On top of the continuous task of increasing the output of a farm was added the new military role to which many farmers and their men had committed themselves. Farm work and war work took up all a man's time, and that of many women as well, and called upon the deepest resources of energy and spirits. The burden of the winter of 1940 was made heavier still by news of the damage the *Luftwaffe* was inflicting on the cities of Britain.

The Grindstone

For the farmers of south-eastern England, the harvest season of 1940 was more hazardous than most. The general wartime situation had provided problems in plenty – a shortage of manpower at a time when farmers had a greatly increased acreage under grain crops, which all had to be harvested within the equivalent few weeks as the lesser crops of previous years; shipping losses in the Atlantic, which hindered the import of the necessary amounts of extra farm machinery from the United States; the supervision or inspection by officials from the local War Agricultural Committee, on behalf of the Ministry of Agriculture, to ensure that the yields of the harvest were up to the targets set and that the best use was being made of all the available manpower and machinery. From mid-summer onwards, the sky over south-east England was segmented by the streams of white vapour left by the exhausts of battling aircraft, and to the singing of birds and the drone of the insect population of hot, sunny days was added the increasing, insistent rumble of hundreds of aircraft engines, as the *Luftwaffe* began their attempt to beat the RAF out of the air.

For weeks the weather was clear and hot, the skies were cloudless and the fields of crops shimmered in the haze. 'Real Battle of Britain weather' people called it in after years. Farmers had cause to remember such weather with less pleasure. Encouraged by the fine summer, holidaymakers attracted by the novelty of the aerial battles over English soil tramped over the fields to marvel at bomb craters, and swarmed around wrecked aircraft picking at them for souvenirs. Few took much notice of the ground they were walking on, whose land it was or what grew on it, and many areas of crops suffered from people trampling them down. The problem grew to such proportions that on one farm twenty-five acres of wheat were destroyed. The

Weariness pervades this lunchtime in the Yorkshire fields. The people's faces are tired; the thin, bony horses tug at a meagre ration of hay.

offence of trampling crops in order to look at wrecked aircraft was made punishable by law, under the threat of a fine of £50 for anyone convicted.

The farmers' difficulties did not end with the crowds. Fields pitted with craters were no use for efficient cultivation, and the holes had to be filled in. The question was, by whom? Neither farmers nor government departments considered themselves solely responsible. Tenant-farmers were told that their responsibility lay only in notifying their landlords about craters or aircraft wrecks on their land. It was an expensive business to refill a large crater, and one area of pastureland in Kent contained ninety-three of them. Landlords enquired of the War Office whether the Government were intending to do anything about the problem. The War Office revealed that troops stationed in nearby camps were allowed to assist with repairs to fields, subject to the discretion of their Commanding Officers, but that it was not the responsibility of the War Office to instruct them to do so.

It was not only crops that suffered. Bombs which went astray, the blast from explosions and, most often, flying shrapnel and machine-gun bullets destroyed many valuable farm animals. The farmer was urged not to waste the meat, however, and had to notify the appropriate local buying authority so that the carcass could be bought from him as quickly as possible and added to the stock of food.

An Italian fighter *above,* obsolete by British and German standards, which crash-landed in a field in Suffolk. The pilot believed that he had been flying over (to him) friendly German territory.

A crater *below* carved out of a field by a Heinkel bomber when it crashed. Farmers, particularly in the south-east of England, were frequently harrassed in this way.

Wrecked German aircraft collected in a Kentish village during the Battle of Britain, being examined for the latest developments in German aeronautics.

Workers on the farms of 'Hell-fire Corner', the south-eastern tip of England, were in the direct line of fire not only of the attacking German aircraft, but also of the shell-fire from the guns on the French coast. Harvesting had to be carried on under the constant threat of machine-gun fire, with the farm workers diving for cover behind tractors and binders whenever German raiders came in for the attack. At such times too, the routines of milking cattle had to be maintained, lest the cattle and the vital milk supply should suffer. Some Land Girls in Hampshire were supplied with tin hats after they had reported frequent danger from shrapnel when they were getting the cows in for milking at 5 o'clock in the morning. Another Land Girl apologised for arriving late for work on a farm near Canterbury, explaining that she had been dug out of the debris of a bombed house.

Although the experiences of harvesting and milking under fire were concentrated in the southern and eastern counties of England, isolated damage from bombing, machine-gunning or crashing aircraft occurred over a wide area of the countryside. But in the overall picture of wartime life in the countryside, these were incidental, if dramatic details. Fundamental to the lives of everyone who worked on the land was the constant and far-reaching planning of land use which affected the working year of every farmer in the land. Such plans had to look some distance into the future, since the time taken between setting a production target for the wheat crop, for instance, and the actual harvesting of that wheat was eighteen months or more.

In spite of the hazards, the harvest of 1940, which was a good one, was brought in. An immediate start was made on preparations for the following year's production, on the lines of production targets already laid down in the summer of 1940. It was obvious by then that the war was not going to be over quickly; that it was not going to reach a compromise solution; and that it was going to be fought bitterly, to the end. There was therefore no question of planning agricultural production so as to maintain the balance of the nation's diet which had relied so much on imports in peacetime.

The campaign to encourage farmers to plough up more grassland was intensified in the winter of 1940. Two and a quarter million extra acres of land were required. Much of this was to be planted with potatoes – enough to supply the needs of the entire British population, even taking into account the possibility of a low yield if the weather were bad in the early autumn of 1941. Sugar-beet production was fixed at a level which would employ the maximum capacity of the

factories which refined the beet into sugar. Suitable districts were designated for a large expansion of the acreage growing vegetables, particularly tomatoes and carrots, to supply vitamins to make up for the loss of imported fruit and vegetables.

The consuming public, of course, had also to make the change from imported foodstuffs to what could be grown at home. Under the auspices of the Ministry of Food, extensive publicity campaigns on the wireless, in the press and on the cinema screen emphasised the virtues of 'Dr Carrot' and 'Potato Pete'. To the eating of carrots, with its consequent improvement in seeing in the dark, was attributed some of the much-publicised success of the fighter pilots who flew against the nightly swarms of German bombers which attacked Britain during the winter of 1940.

Briefly in 1940 plans for shifting the public diet into primarily home-grown foodstuffs received a set-back, when, with the closure of European ports by the occupying German forces, a number of cargoes originally bound for Europe were diverted to British ports. Although the increase in imports was short-lived, it stayed the Government's hand in forcing far-reaching and probably unpopular measures which would mean ordering many farmers radically to alter their ways of farming their land.

Farmers who were willing enough to plough up the grassland required were not helped by the weather. November 1940 was particularly wet and prevented good progress with autumn ploughing. No work could be done on the fields until March, because of heavy snowfalls and severe frosts. At the other end of the season the weather at harvest-time was unsettled and the gathering of the crops was frequently interrupted by rain. But despite all the difficulties the yields were good. In the Midlands great areas of land had grown wheat and potatoes where for years the fields had been used only as grazing land. Similarly, in counties up the west coast of England, which had been given over almost entirely to dairy farming, the fields provided good yields of oats and kale to supply winter feed for cattle, which was now unobtainable from abroad.

On the other hand, the movement to arable farming inevitably meant a temporary decrease in the number of cattle supplying milk. Much of what was available was converted into condensed milk for storage and use by the Forces. Through vigorous advertising campaigns extolling the health-giving properties of milk, the demand was rising. The overriding importance of the production of wheat and potatoes, however, meant that only the top priority users of liquid milk under the National Milk Scheme – pregnant women, babies and

Sarrat ARP centre *above* in operation. The post covered a rural area of south-west Hertfordshire.
Caves *below* in the cliffs near Dover provided shelter from the shelling by German guns on the French coast.

Near Waltham Abbey *right* German bombs cause catastrophe and chaos. Fire and rescue services struggle to free the bodies of the dead and injured.

PLOUGH NOW!
by day and night

GROW FOOD FOR THE NATION
FEEDING STUFFS FOR YOUR FARMS
KEEP OUR SHIPS AND MONEY FREE
FOR BUYING VITAL ARMS

★THE PRIME MINISTER TO FARMERS AND WORKERS—

The Prime Minister, speaking on February 28th :

"The Minister of Agriculture made a pronouncement last December, when he said : 'If the increase in home production that we want is to be obtained, then the prices must be such as would give a reasonable return to the farmer and enable the farmer to pay a fair wage to the worker.' I want to say again that the War Cabinet endorses that declaration by the Minister of Agriculture."

infants – were assured of a regular supply. In many towns there were shortages in the winter of 1940; restrictions were imposed on the distribution of liquid milk in April 1941 and during the year plans for full rationing of milk were formulated.

As soon as crops had been sown in the winter of 1941, plans were being laid for the crops to be planted in the winter of 1942 and the spring of 1943, which would be harvested in the autumn of 1943, for the consumption of the population in 1944. Under the circumstances of war, this was looking a long way ahead. No-one could tell with certainty what the course of the war would be. The planning of agricultural production had to be integrated with long-term military strategy, since the amount of food for human and animal consumption produced at home was closely related to the amount which could be imported. This figure depended partly on the progress of the naval war in the Atlantic, and partly on the date of the Allied invasion of Europe, when vast amounts of shipping space would be needed to ferry troops and equipment across the channel from southern England.

In December, 1941, such an invasion seemed a remote prospect indeed. The entry of the United States into the war was only a few days old, and al-

The urgency of the ploughing campaign was emphasised by the message of this poster *left. Below* a Land Army girl at work ploughing fields by night.

though it turned the balance of advantage in favour of the Allies' ultimate victory, it was recognised that there were still years of bitter fighting abroad, and stringent conditions at home, to be suffered before that victory was achieved. Nevertheless, the agricultural planners had to work on such long-term considerations, and made a hopeful guess that the invasion of France by the Allies would take place in the summer of 1943, with a possibility that it would be delayed until 1944. On this premise they intended that the peak of agricultural output in terms of the tonnage of crops harvested should be reached at the harvest of 1943.

The comparison with pre-war production was startling: 9½ million acres of corn were to be sown, compared with 5¼ million acres in 1939. Added to this were another half million acres of potatoes and sugar-beet. The Ministry of Food was particularly concerned that potatoes should not be rationed, and that the supply, even on the average yields of the poorest years, should nevertheless keep pace with demand. Potatoes yielded more calories per acre than wheat, and publicity campaigns were highly effective in persuading the public to eat more. What was only fully realised when statistics were analysed was that potatoes were subject to a very high rate of wastage, through blight or other causes, and of the 1944 crop only 6 million out of the 10 million tons of potatoes lifted were fit for consumption. Nevertheless consumption of potatoes continued to be encouraged and their nutritional value emphasised.

By the time these plans were finalised, in the spring of 1942, cultivation at ever-increasing intensity had been going on in British farms for 3, maybe 4 years. Agricultural land, unless it is exceptional, can only bear heavy crops of one sort for 2 or 3 years. After that repeated sowings of the same crop yield less and less at harvest and are subject to an increasing degree of weed and pest infestation. The land has to rest and be re-fertilised, usually by turning it into temporary pasture and grazing cattle and sheep on it. Rotation of crops and pasture was a time-honoured practice, developed through centuries of mixed farming, and no war for the salvation of civilisation was going to change its validity. If the land were not to be worked to the death, with its consequence of severe shortages of cereal crops in 1945 or 1946, new land had to be found which could be ploughed up, so that the present land under grain crops or potatoes could be returned to a state of temporary pasture.

The supply of fresh grassland to be turned into arable land was very short indeed. Since the beginning of the war, 5 million acres of grassland had been ploughed under. What was left was the worst of what had been available. Ploughs would have to be dragged

Within twelve months of being derelict land, this field at Fambridge, Essex was producing good crops of oats, under the aegis of the War Agricultural Committee.

further up hillsides where steepening slopes and the thinness of the soil made work difficult and unrewarding; or on to poorer soils which were thick with weed and bracken; or into marshier, wet ground which would first have to be expensively drained. The War Agricultural Committees estimated the amount of grassland which could be ploughed up and be expected to yield a reasonable first crop of wheat or potatoes in the summer of 1942 to be another half a million acres. Beyond that area the land was of marginal value and it was doubtful whether the price received by the farmer for the crop grown would cover the expense of breaking up and preparing the land; it was obviously not possible for a farmer to subsidise the nation by producing food at a loss to himself.

In spite of the American entry into the war in December 1941, the following year showed no marked advance in the Allies' fortunes. Shipping losses were still heavy. Much American cargo space was devoted to the war in the Pacific. In order to maintain the supply of bread (which was not rationed) in the shops of Britain, the wheat which went into making its flour was supplemented with other cereals, such as rye, barley and oats. The supply of wheat was not to be reduced, but more rye, barley and oats had to be grown. But this had not to be at the expense of the crops of potatoes, sugar beet and flax which all had to be maintained at their previous levels. The War Agricultural Committees were firmly asked by the Ministry of Agriculture to find another million acres of grassland to be ploughed to bear the extra crops. The profitability of the extra crops was open to doubt. By 1942 this was a secondary matter, as the Government recognised the paramount necessity of achieving, whatever the cost, the maximum possible supply of basic foodstuffs from the farms of Britain.

The War Agricultural Committees had the powers of compulsion necessary to achieve such a level of production but not to alleviate the costs, which had to be borne by the farmer out of the price the Government was prepared to pay for the produce he grew. This was fixed at a high rate at the beginning of the war, in order to encourage farmers to produce the wheat required. As the production of wheat increased, however, the expense of producing it did not fall, as it might have done in a mechanical industry, but often rose. To prepare for a second crop of wheat on land which had already borne one entailed ploughing, cultivating and dragging the land a number of times in order to clean it as soon as the first crop had been harvested. Land which had spent some time under grass did not need the extensive manuring operation which land intended to bear a crop of wheat two years in succession had to undergo. All these operations took time and money.

Farmers in eastern counties of England, traditional wheat-growing areas, were not under such great

Canadian sailors detailed onto a farm as supplementary labour to help with the sheep-dipping, enabling the farmer to get on with other jobs.

pressure as those in the west, where dairying, which needed large areas of grassland, was the predominant form of agriculture. In East Anglia the composition of the soil was such that it could bear 2 or even 3 successive wheat crops without too great a diminution of its fertility. In the western counties frequent manuring by grazing cattle on land which was temporarily given over to grass was thought necessary to the most economical production of good-quality crops. In areas of this type the debate was sharpest between the War Agricultural Committee members, who had to find the extra arable acreage to increase the supply of wheat, and their farming neighbours who were dubious about the effect of over-production on their land.

Worries about over-production and the decline in fertility of the soil were aggravated by the increasing deficiency in supplies of fertilisers, many of which were imported from abroad. One of the most important was potash, which was used extensively to fertilise fields for the production of potatoes, sugar beet, root vegetables and flax. Previously half the nation's supply had come from Germany and Alsace. On the outbreak of war the quantity coming into the country was thus reduced by fifty per cent, and the amount available

The potato harvest from Aston Down airfield being gathered in by airmen and WAAFs.

did not greatly improve until 1944. With supplies so short, it was made illegal to use potash on any land which was not going to be used for the vital crops which needed it, or for land which had been certified by the War Agricultural Committee as particularly deficient in potash.

Fertilisers made from phosphates were obtained partly from basic slag, the waste material from the steel-making process. Since the production of steel was on the increase, partial supplies of phosphates were not difficult to come by. As with potash, however, the rest was imported. Supplies from North America ceased after 1940; alternative supplies from Pacific islands, far more expensive because of the transport involved, were cut off by the entry of Japan into the war. Imports from the United States were insufficient for the needs of British farmers. Old grassland, which farmers were repeatedly required to plough up and turn into arable land, was often seriously deficient in phosphates and lime and the amount farmers put into the land as a dressing was often not enough to ensure a good first crop of corn. Lime was home-produced and production was quickly increased, but supplies of phosphates and potash were rationed in 1942 so that

each area received fertilisers in proportion to the amount of arable land it possessed.

Diminishing the acreage of grassland in order to plough it up for crop production also implied the slaughtering of the cattle which could no longer be fed from the smaller acreage of pasture. On the majority of farms the problems were overcome or put up with in the spurt of wartime co-operation which remains so prominently in the memories of those who partook in or felt the benefit of it. In general the War Agricultural Committees left to the individual farmer the decision as to the number of livestock he was able to maintain on a farm with a diminished acreage of grassland. Many cattle and sheep were of necessity slaughtered, but on some farms more carefully controlled grazing actually led to an increase in the number of animals, as well as the required increase in output of crops.

The difficulties of stock farming were not eased by the introduction of rationing of feeding stuffs for livestock. The scheme was planned in the autumn of 1940, but only then because of the startling increase in shipping losses in the Atlantic during the summer months. The need for some sort of control had been recognised from the outset of the war, but the complexity of the problem and the hope that the increase in the home production of animal fodder in the harvest of 1940 would fill the gap left by the drop in imports had not prompted an immediate solution. The worsen-

ing shipping situation, the fact that an end to the war looked a distant prospect, and the increasing demand for milk, putting pressure on dairy farmers to maintain if not increase the yield from each of their animals, all made rationing essential.

The rationing of animal feedstuffs was cumbrous and complicated. For each sort of animal nutritionists calculated a 'maintenance ration' – the amount of food it would need simply to keep it alive – and a 'production ration', which was the food in the form of starch and protein which enabled dairy cows to provide milk and animals such as pigs to get fatter and thus provide meat. It was assumed that the maintenance ration could be met by the farm's own production of hay, straw and root and fodder crops. Cereals, pulse and cattle cake would supply the productive ration. Farmers whose holdings did not grow enough of these latter crops to satisfy the animals' needs were entitled to coupons which allowed them to buy extra food from a merchant, with whom he had to register.

The clerical administration involved was vast. The Department of Agriculture in Scotland and the War Agricultural Committees in England and Wales had to compile the number of cattle, sheep, horses, pigs and poultry each individual farm possessed, how much milk each cow produced, since this was included in the calculation of its ration, how much of the farm was under cultivation and with what crops. The

Camouflaging nets, *above* to be used to protect vehicles or guns from aerial reconnaissance, was a slow job.

A working party *below* gathered in a Cornish fisherman's institute, sewing on behalf of the Red Cross.

The WVS Pie Scheme was officially adopted by the Ministry of Food in 1942. In rural areas, rations were supplemented by selling pies and snacks to farm workers. Nearly one and a half million pies were sold each week.

rationing scheme was scheduled to begin at the beginning of 1941. In fact it came into force in the February, and then only by dint of long hours of arduous work on the part of those who compiled the statistics and calculated the rations.

The introduction of the scheme in February caused innumerable problems, since it was the middle of the farming year, and many transactions of crops and stock had already taken place and had to be accounted for in calculating a farmer's present stockholding of animal foodstuffs and his future needs. Further complications were introduced by classing farmers as 'surplus' or 'deficit' farmers, depending on whether the estimated production of their fodder crops was going to be more or less than their calculated feed requirements.

The scheme was given a much-needed overhaul and simplification in 1941, when 'surplus' and 'deficit' categories were abolished and rations for animals were restricted to dairy cows, pigs and poultry. The milk yields were easily measured. The numbers of pigs and poultry to be fed were based on a fraction of the actual numbers on each farm, which were already known. The administration of the rationing scheme was much eased and discrepancies or special circumstances could

be adjusted for locally by the allowance of a small surplus to the calculated requirement to each county's War Agricultural Committee, who dispensed it as they saw fit.

To the general consumer in Britain's cities and towns, the agricultural production campaign presented fairly straightforward problems which were capable of obvious solutions, although involving a great deal of hard work. 'Dig for Victory' in the towns meant a number of hours' heavy toil with a fork and spade, a bit of planting and weeding, and harvesting a small crop of vegetables at the due season. Outwardly, the farmers' problems appeared essentially the same; only the scale differed. The nation's city dwellers, by far the majority of the population, knew through the press that farmers were being asked to plough up millions of acres of land uncultivated for many years, perhaps hundreds of years, and that many of those acres had been employed since the Great War in feeding cattle and other live-stock. The equation then seemed simple: fewer cattle meant more crops. The nation was apparently pre-pared to put up with less meat for the sake of un-rationed bread and the saving of imported food.

In a sense, a number of farmers agreed, and in the autumn of 1940 large numbers of animals which had been fattened off the rich summer grass, and, in the south-east, animals which had come under direct fire from the enemy, were sent to the slaughterhouses.

The community was endlessly asked to raise money to fund the Government's wartime expenditure. *Above* National Savings were vigorously encouraged. *Below* Aluminium collected by the village of Cuffley, Hertfordshire. The 'Cuffley Zepp', noted on the right, was a zeppelin which crashed nearby in the First World War. *Centre left* Posters renewed the constant exhortation to lend money to the Government. *Centre right* £100,000 was the target for Abingdon's War Weapons Week. *Bottom right* Emett's cartoon is just a slight exaggeration of the reality *above right* of the fund-raising campaigns which left no corner of the country undisturbed or untapped.

Be wise!

LEND TO DEFEND

"*I wish they could have lent us a Lancaster . . .*"

Sugar beet being thinned by boys from Lewes County school in Sussex.

The sudden great influx of animals which heavily overburdened the Ministry of Agriculture's slaughtering facilities created a sharp controversy.

The slaughtering drastically reduced the population of farm animals, particularly of cattle and sheep, thereby depleting stocks of 'meat on the hoof' for consumption the following year. Many people contended that the British were a meat eating nation; that if there were no roast beef then morale would seriously suffer. A more pertinent argument came from agriculturalists who believed that farmland would suffer seriously if livestock numbers were too heavily depleted. Until the retrenchment in arable farming between the wars, British farming had been broadly based on the principles of the mixed farm, in livestock fed on the by-products of corn and roots supplemented by concentrated cattlefeed, and the manure they produced was used to fertilise the fields for new crops of wheat, followed frequently by barley, oats and potatoes. The rotation system was hallowed by time and experience, and the heavy slaughtering of cattle seemed to endanger its life.

On the other side were the arguments of the nutritional experts and the dire level of food stocks caused by the increase in the number of merchant ships bringing food into Britain being sunk by German U-boats. The information and advice provided by nutritional scientists had gained in authority during the late 1930s and formed the basis for much of the food rationing and control policy of the Ministry of Food throughout the war. In theory, the nutritional needs of the nation could be met by a diet composed solely of wholemeal bread, oatmeal, fats, milk, potatoes and vegetables. In practice such a diet was not possible to provide, since enough oatmeal could not be produced by the British mills. From the point of view of the people, a diet of this nature would be a drastic departure from the normal everyday meal, and it was felt that a quick or sudden change into it might have a serious effect on the people's morale and will to resist attack. However, in spite of the extra meat in store in the winter of 1940, due to the heavy slaughtering of the autumn, the rate of shipping losses was such that supplies of meat from Argentina were virtually cut off, and in the spring of 1941 the meat ration fell to one shilling's worth per person per week. Although there were the inevitable grumbles, there was no apparent diminution in the public's capacity to withstand the bombing attacks, the propaganda war, or the endless hours of sheer hard work they were prepared to undergo in order to turn out ever more arms and equipment to stem the Nazi advance to their attempted domination of the world.

The comparatively harmless effect of the shortage of meat from abroad, the fact that the nation could be nutritionally supplied without it, and the desperate need for basic cereal and vegetable foodstuffs led to government advice to farmers to do with still fewer livestock, maintaining only those which could effectively use the available feeding stuffs for milk production and to turn into meat the by-products of the cultivation of corn and root vegetables. Between the autumn of 1940 and 1942, the numbers of livestock on British farms were extensively, if erratically, reduced. The favoured time of year for selling off cattle to be slaughtered was after they had fattened, following a summer of grazing on rich pastures. It would have been more helpful to the Ministry of Food if the flow of livestock being slaughtered had been much more even. If stock had been slaughtered in March 1941, for instance, when the shortage of meat was most severe, the yield of meat from each beast would have been low since they would not yet have reached their peak of fatness and thus the most economical and efficient time at which to slaughter them for their meat. The relationship between cattle and their fodder supplies is a complex one and because each farmer had different acreages of grassland and arable land under fodder crops, it was left to the individual farmer and his local War Agricultural Committee to come to the final decision as to how many cattle his land could support.

Another crop for which demand suddenly increased was flax. In the autumn of 1941 the Ministry of

The Army and the RAF helping with the threshing during the harvest time of 1942.

Supply was pleading with the agriculturalists in Whitehall to order that 150,000 acres of flax be planted. Previously Britain's principal supplies of flax had come from the Baltic States, but this source was now obviously cut off. Flax provides a tough vegetable fibre, which, in its finest form, is used to make linen. The coarser varieties were used during the war to make webbing for parachute harnesses, fire hoses, gun tarpaulins and the thread used in sewing military boots. Flax needs a highly fertile soil and plenty of rainfall, which made it suitable for growing in a number of districts in the western areas of Britain. Many farmers were reluctant to undertake the production of flax, however, because mechanisation of the means of harvesting flax was still at an early stage and without machines, the flax plants had to be pulled by hand. After pulling, the fibre had to be separated from the stem, which involved a laborious process of soaking and drying. Machines for carrying out these processes were developed during the war, but the War Agricultural Committees who directed farmers to grow flax were never the most popular men.

The demand for increased crop production caused

problems not only at the beginning of the farmer's year, when he had to decide the level of his livestock holding, and plough his fields, but at harvest-time as well. The seasons allowed no more time for harvesting a crop grown over a large area of land than they did over a small acreage. When the wartime crops were to be harvested it was even more essential than ever that the few vital weeks at the end of the summer should be filled with fair weather. It was a strange fact of the wartime years that, overall, farmers were outstandingly lucky with their harvest weather. Fine summers from 1939 to 1943 meant that records for crop yields were broken annually.

Luck could play no part in the supply of labour, which was strictly regulated by the Ministry of Labour. Although from 1940 unemployed men could be directed into agricultural employment, and those already working on the land were required to stay in their occupations, the call-up into the Forces and the initial wave of workers who left agricultural employment in order to take up better-paid jobs in the new or converted factories making military supplies and munitions had considerably depleted the labour force. It was far

more difficult to persuade or even to find the men able to move back to the land. National Service for women aged twenty to thirty was introduced in December 1941 and eventually to cover women between the ages of eighteen and fifty years. Many of these women volunteered to join the WLA, and many farmers found themselves dependent upon the work of the WLA. After a bumper harvest in 1942, and further plans for expansion in 1943, a recruitment drive was launched to find further men or women to work on the land, but few came forward. By this time the entire nation had been mobilised, and were serving either in the Forces, in civil defence work, in civilian employment directly concerned with war production, or in other industries supplying the basic needs of the population. The nation's labour force was controlled and could be moved in any direction that the course of the war demanded. But that course over-rigidly demanded a concentrated effort to produce ever more armaments and military equipment. There were no more pairs of hands left over to work permanently on the land.

For much of their harvest-time labour farmers had to rely on casual workers. Mechanisation of the harvesting of corn, particularly in the East Anglian counties which had broader, more open fields more suitable for working by machines, eased the difficulties to some extent. The farmer's greatest headache was lifting the

Ricking hay on an LCC farm in Chipstead. The horse-powered elevator gear went out of common use in the 1890s, but returned to play its part in wartime agriculture.

A combine harvester, little more than a trailer with traditional machinery grouped upon it, in operation in Hampshire in 1940. An early model such as this needed three men to run it.

potato crop, which required many hands and many hours of manual labour. In the harvest of 1943, nearly 10 million tons of potatoes had to be lifted, sorted into bags for sale, or else stored and bagged at a later date. All these operations were carried out by hand.

This need for high numbers of workers carrying out jobs concentrated into a short period of time caused problems of production which were largely unforeseen at the time crops were planted, and were only revealed in the light of experience. One particular farmer in Wiltshire never grew potatoes before the war and had concentrated a fair proportion of his output on growing high quality wheat for sale to a seed-merchant, who would resell the seed for planting as wheat the following year, rather than milling the grain into flour. The increased targets for potato production ordained by the Ministry of Agriculture had caused the local War Agricultural Committee to order the farmer to grow a crop of potatoes. The configuration of the farm meant that potatoes had to be grown on heavy land and the entire workforce on the farm had to spend a week of the harvest season picking them. Although the potatoes were a profitable crop, the farmer lost money overall because the time taken to harvest the potatoes

had eaten into the period normally set aside for threshing the crop of wheat. The threshing could not be done earlier, because the wheat needed to stand for a certain time in a rick before it could be properly threshed to provide a sample of the seed. Following the potato-picking, the farmer was engaged on ploughing his fields for the following year's crops. Although some of the wheat was threshed in time to meet a time of peak demand and highest price the rest had to be sold for 10 shillings less per quarter. Experiences such as these led this farmer to consider ever more carefully the ways in which his staff could be used most effectively and which crops should be grown to employ the available time to the fullest advantage. The order to sow potatoes had come after his crop of wheat was sown. Had it come before, the farmer would have sown a wheat to be used for milling rather than for seed, since the time for threshing and the premium the corn merchant was prepared to pay when he wanted the wheat most would have been less critical factors.

The casual labour on which the farmers had to rely came from a number of sources. Local people from villages or neighbouring farms helped out when they could, but frequently their own needs for assistance were just as great. School-children living in the area or who had been evacuated from the cities were often organised into gangs to help with potato planting and lifting. Children in secondary schools who were not

Harvesting *above* carried out by Italian prisoners-of-war under the eye of their guarding corporal.

Hand-binding *left* of corn by soldiers following the cutter in difficult terrain in the Lake District.

Queen Mary *below* visiting holidaymakers from the cities who had decided to spend their annual holiday working on the land.

concerned with examinations were given a week off to assist in the potato harvest. Buses collected them, with their teachers, from the school gates in the morning and deposited them in the evening after a strenuous day's work. A vigorous poster and wireless campaign in the towns, exhorting people to 'Lend a hand on the land', produced an enthusiastic response which led to the institution of a number of camps to house these temporary workers. Organised by the War Agricultural Committees, they provided board and lodging for families from the towns who chose to spend their week or fortnight's holiday in the countryside, helping the war effort in a way which was probably the complete antithesis of their occupation throughout the rest of the year. By the end of the war, the numbers of casual labourers had been swollen by the prisoners of war who were allowed out of their camps under armed guard to work on the farms.

Farmers had tried to alleviate the labour problem a little by mechanising their operations, using one man on a tractor to draw a plough, for example, where before a number of ploughmen with teams of horses would have done the job. One major disadvantage was that unlike the horses' fodder, fuel for the tractor could not be grown on the farm and petrol was subject to stringent rationing.

Petrol rationing began for private motorists almost as soon as the war started. Depending upon the size of the car and its engine's horsepower, the ration was enough for an average of 150 miles' motoring a month. Cuts came in the ration in the autumn of 1941 and spring of 1942. From 1 July 1942, the private motorist's ration disappeared altogether.

The waning of the private petrol ration reflected the worsening shortage of petrol in the country as a

Commercial advertising often included elements of national propaganda. The system of controlled distribution meant that, in rotation, areas of the country might be without supplies of a commodity for long periods.

whole. It was one of the commodities most seriously affected by the losses of merchant shipping since Britain had no crude oil resources of her own which could be refined into petrol. The situation was made more critical, both for the private and for the industrial consumer, by the increasing needs of the Forces, particularly the RAF, whose bomber offensive against German cities and industries used ever-increasing amounts of fuel. The proportion of the military to the private use of fuel was colossal anyway. One average flight in a Spitfire used the same amount of fuel as was allowed to a private motorist for a year's motoring.

To the people of the countryside who had cars, which was a comparatively small number, since at the outbreak of war there were only 2 million private vehicles on the roads of Britain, petrol rationing came as a great blow, since they had often begun to rely on a motor-car as their principal means of transport. The majority of people did not own a car and were affected by the restrictions only indirectly, through the cuts in public transport.

Farmers themselves were able to claim special allowances of fuel. The rations were far from generous however, and every precious gallon had to be carefully used. Such extra rations did allow of one or two shopping expeditions or trips to the cinema in the local town, if some spurious business reason could be concocted to satisfy any inquisitive policeman who, as he was entitled to do, might check into the purpose of the journey. As the Battle of the Atlantic, in which the German U-boats did so much damage to Allied merchant shipping, reached a critical phase, such brief, domestic pleasure trips became more and more rare.

During 1941 Allied shipping suffered severe losses. At the end of the year the Japanese attacked Pearl Harbour and brought the United States into the war, thus making it a truly global conflict. Although the Japanese attack confirmed the United States as Britain's ally, this did not immediately ease the position with regard to the blockade. In fact the war at sea intensified, and German U-boats felt themselves free to attack unprotected shipping in the western Atlantic, which until that time they had refrained from doing. The war in the Pacific increased the burden on American and British shipping still further, since the two nations' maritime transport capacity was stretched even further. During most of 1942 more British ships were sunk than there were new ships being built. Only at the end of the year did production overtake destruction, but then the new ships were immediately pressed into service to carry troops and equipment to North Africa, Sicily, Italy and the Far East.

The catch brought ashore, fished from the dangerous waters of the North Sea, the men forever on the lookout against attacks from German E-boats and aircraft.

A **trawler** converted for minesweeping duties, with sweeping gear attached to the bows. An anti-aircraft gun has been mounted over the foredeck and the bridge has been given protective covering against machine-gun fire from enemy aircraft.

As far as British agriculture was concerned, the outcome was a further decrease in the supplies of cereals and foodstuffs for human and animal consumption. The shipping losses and the entry of the United States into the war also slowed the rate of mechanisation of British farming. The American factories which had been turning out tractors, ploughs, combine harvesters and other agricultural machinery for export to Britain were converted to produce machinery more appropriate to the needs of the US army. The Japanese conquest of south-east Asia led to a severe shortage of rubber which meant that tractor-wheels, for instance, had to be made of steel, of which there was little enough to meet the huge demand of the armaments industries of both Britain and the United States.

The maritime blockade led to a new role for many of Britain's fishing vessels. A number of deep-sea trawlers were converted for use as anti-submarine vessels and for mine-sweeping duties. They were armed with 4-inch guns and smaller automatic weapons, mainly as a defence against air attack.

The difficulty of navigation in the North Sea and the increasing effectiveness of British sea and air defences meant that U-boats became less common in these waters. The trawlers which patrolled the waters against the U-boats took on rescue and salvage operations in the convoys of merchant ships which passed up and down the Channel and out into the Atlantic. Their duties lay principally in getting bombed ships out of the sea-lanes used by the convoys, and picking up survivors from them. When on night patrol, armed trawlers were ordered to hold up any merchant ship which was sailing unescorted to ensure that enemy ships were not slipping into the convoy routes and seeding them with mines. Patrols were carried out about fifteen to twenty-five miles off the British coast, beginning at dusk and ending the following morning. Air attacks from German bombers or fighters were frequent. In the early skirmishes trawlers would blaze away at aircraft with their machine-guns until their ammunition was spent. The enemy aircraft would then attack from a few hundred feet, returning again and again until the now defenceless ship was sunk. Gradually the trawler crews gained experience, and held their fire until the last possible moment in the hope of bringing down the aircraft with a direct hit. Sometimes they succeeded; at other times the aircraft would turn away, having failed to achieve its object.

The mouths of the ports of Britain were also extensively mined by German aircraft and E-boats, and the peacetime fishing fleet was closely engaged in mine-

'The Boyhood of Raleigh' *above* given a wartime flavour as evacuees sit at the feet of an old salt in Brixham, Devon.

Nets hauled in *below* whilst a Lewis gun is being stripped and cleaned – the two aspects of wartime fishing, vital to Britain's food supply.

sweeping operations. Some craft searched out moored mines, which usually lay about eighteen feet below the surface of the sea. A serrated wire attached to a torpedo-shaped float which was sent out from the trawler was intended to pass beneath the mine, sever its mooring and send it to the surface, where it would be exploded or sunk by gunfire from a pursuing vessel. The trawlers often operated in groups, sweeping a wide channel ahead of an approaching convoy or particularly valuable warship passing around the coast of Britain. Amongst a convoy, unarmed trawlers, going about their business of fishing, might take shelter steaming to or from their fishing grounds with the comparative safety afforded by a naval escort and air cover from the RAF.

The crews of the armed trawlers were frequently members of the Royal Naval Voluntary Reserve. While the captain was probably a life-long deep sea fisherman, his crew could have been drawn from any occupation in the land. Grocers and fruiterers, bricklayers and upholsterers, plasterers and plumbers manned the guns, the engines and the navigational equipment of the converted trawlers. Their efforts in protecting the convoys from the dangers of mined waters and attack from the air maintained a vital link in the chain of supplies coming into Britain, without which her industry and her agriculture would have ground to a halt.

The Fat of the Land

Sitting at the edge of a field of ripening wheat, on a balmy day with just a few flimsy white clouds brushed across the blue sky, overlooking a patchwork green expanse of the fertile English countryside, the physical terrors and the anguish of war must have seemed to belong to a completely different world. Late on a dark, bitter night, with black, stark trees standing out against thick snow, a shepherd concentrating on helping his ewes to bring new lambs into the world must have thought the shooting and the bombing and the carnage equally remote. Children evacuated from the cities, having taken stock of their new, rural surroundings,

were heard to remark, 'There's no war on here'. Most parts of the countryside were officially regarded as a haven, by the evacuating authorities; for many people, residents or visitors, they were just that.

Restrictions there undoubtedly were. The shortage of petrol caused considerable difficulties to farmers and to such people as country doctors, who needed their cars to maintain their care for their patients. Country housewives were pestered as much as city dwellers by ration books and the regulations concerning coupons and the points rationing scheme. The stream of government pamphlets about blackout precautions,

the carrying of gas masks, protection of the home against air attack and advice on how to act in the event of an invasion was no less of a torrent through rural letter boxes than it was in the city.

In the majority of small towns and villages, the war did not approach much nearer as far as daily life was concerned. Away from the southern and East Anglian coasts, the sight of an invading army, headed by fearsome paratroopers and the swift, deadly, armoured vehicles of the renowned Panzer divisions, approaching along leafy lanes or through apple-laden orchards which had stood peacefully for decades was virtually unimaginable. Very few villages suffered the shock, the damage and the distress caused by bombing or bombardment from the coastal batteries on the French shore of the Channel. In some areas of the country enemy planes were often seen overhead, on their way to some urban or industrial target. In the south and along the eastern coast dogfights between the RAF and the *Luftwaffe* were watched with interest and excitement from the fields. But direct physical experience of the battles over and around Britain was not the general rule in the countryside. News came through, on the wireless or in the newspapers, of battles fought on the sea and in the air for the survival of Britain and its people. The people rejoiced or were saddened at what they were told, but the uninterrupted business of the day was paramount. As one farmer said, 'The war is only a sideshow after all. The real show is the farm.'

The years of war were perhaps some of the best times to visit the countryside. As the nation's petrol ration gradually diminished, cars on the country roads virtually disappeared. The lanes and country roads became a paradise for hikers and cyclists. With the beaches at the coastal resorts either closed or so covered with barbed wire, iron spikes and other anti-invasion devices that to sit amongst them was to be surrounded by harsh reminders of the war, many more people turned to the inland countryside for their recreation. A number of them volunteered to help with the business of farming, particularly at harvest time. Since travel was difficult, many explored in detail parts of the countryside which they might otherwise only have passed through. For men and women who were in the Forces or their auxiliary services, often a brief leave of 2 or 3 days, maybe just a weekend, was all they were able to take. Memories of peaceful hours away from the tension and regulation of war were dearly treasured back on duty.

For certain sections of the population, weekends in the country had been a favourite pastime during the 1920s and 1930s. People who owned large country

'**Sheep may safely graze**' as long as the alert is not sounded.

English ladies offer the hospitality of tea in the parlour to US Army officers stationed at Winchester.

houses would throw house parties, to which they would invite an assortment of guests to stay for the weekend. It was a fashionable occupation, and the round of visits to sociable country houses within a reasonable distance of London amused those who partook of its pleasures, and those who enjoyed them vicariously through the flattery or criticism purveyed in the gossip columns of the newspapers.

To maintain a similar social round in wartime was felt by some to be good for the spirits; by others to be unpatriotic and extravagant. It went against the advice of the Government, as did all holiday travel, to undertake no journeys which were not strictly necessary. To ignore government advice in a matter which might cause discomfort through overcrowding transport, but no real danger, was often felt to be no bad thing. Holidays, whether they were house-parties in a mansion or bed and breakfast in a country pub, were symbols of defiance to the enemy and people were determined to make the most of them.

For the weekending house-parties, circumstances forced a contraction of their activities. Many members of their circles were called up into the Forces, and such

weekend delights, except upon rare occasions, became simply memories of past gaiety. The staff required to run a country house was also severely depleted by the call-up and by the movement of men and women away from inessential occupations into industries producing arms and military equipment. Many houses were closed, their owners remaining in London or in smaller houses elsewhere in the country. A number of country houses were commandeered by the Government, either as permanent bases for government departments for the duration of the war or as precautionary measures in case a retreat from London became necessary in the face of a powerful invading force. Others were turned into hospitals; some were used as hostels for ARP Civil Defence workers, exhausted from their labours in the bombed cities.

Free or assisted holidays were available in later years of the war to such groups of people, and many were pleased to escape from the rubble, broken glass, ruined buildings and derelict houses of the worst areas of the damaged cities. Some guests from the cities on recuperative holidays stayed in country houses where their owners lived, being beyond retirement age, or involved with war work in their locality. Such arrangements often worked well, to the mutual enjoyment of both parties.

There were, no doubt, exceptions. Some people living in safety in the countryside thought themselves by birth, right or fortune, lucky to be doing so and that the rest of the population had simply not been as lucky as they. These were usually the thorns in the flesh of a billeting officer's life, people with large houses and ample incomes who refused to share their precious, enclosed peace with anyone else, however worthy their claim for assistance or consideration. Although they could be compelled to take evacuees, the children or women billeted upon them were made to feel most unwelcome and left as soon as they could. Houseowners with property to let in the safety zones of the country were tempted, early in the war, to cash in on the desires of people who wished to move out of the cities, to escape the air attacks. Advertisements for furnished cottages and sheltered farmhouses proliferated in the more expensive newspapers, and drew down much criticism on those who, because they could afford to, were fleeing from a possible danger which others were forced to endure. Equally vilified were those who took up residence in hotels which advertised themselves as sanctuaries where aero engines were rarely heard, and the sound of an airraid siren was unknown. The residents were castigated as rich refugees, who did nothing but consume food

Harewood House, home of the Princess Royal, converted into a hospital for military personnel, provided elegant surroundings in which to recover.

The WLA taking part in a Warship Week Parade in Wadebridge, Cornwall.

and drink, read and knit, as the war took its course as far away from themselves as they could manage to keep it.

In some ways the demise of the country house-party habit and the retreat of the rich refugees were the outward signs of the disappearance, not so much of an aristocratic or *haut bourgeois* group of people, but of a publicity-conscious way of life which they pursued. At its most extreme in the 1920s, and living on through the next decade, the overbrimming public self-assurance and self-amusement of monied, leisured families was tempered during the war. Indiscriminate suffering from air attack, and an enemy common to every man, woman and child in the country to be fought, played a large part in the process. A sense of social responsibility grew which differed from the lingering Victorian ideal of benign but despotic paternalism of the employer towards his employees. It was based on a genuinely wider recognition of the shared qualities of all men and women, whatever their birth and background. The paternalism was slowly channelled into state institutions, which seemed the only way to retain what was good and dispose of what was bad in the old system.

In the countryside the change was not so marked.

The social upheaval, although extensive, was not as great as in the cities, since the basis of rural society, the agriculture, underwent no radical change, only a change in degree and emphasis. What new influences there were tended to be temporary, arising from the passing presence of evacuees from the cities, or the camps of foreign servicemen, usually from across the Atlantic, in slow transit to the war in Europe. So the social hierarchy in the countryside remained, and to a lesser extent remains today, as it was before the war. The difference between the urban rich and the rural rich was that in general the rural 'county' community was less prone to newspaper and magazine publicity outside its own immediate area than the 'gay young things' and their successors in the towns. The war didn't change these people greatly in themselves; rather, it changed the amount of notice taken of them, by the majority of the population.

As well as the indiscriminate aerial attacks, to which the whole population might be subjected, every man, woman and child in the country was confronted by the problem of food rationing. In spite of some opposition in the press and the Government's hesitancy in introducing the scheme, rationing was generally approved of. This approval was part of an undeniably egalitarian sentiment which pervaded most social dealings during the war. Rationing was called for, not so much from a fear that food would run out, but more out of a feeling

Woollens from Australia *above* distributed by the WVS at a hall in the south of England. *Below* A vigorous fund-raising campaign for the Bodmin Hospital

that if the very survival of the British nation were threatened by an external enemy, then the burden of the struggle should be borne equally by all members of the population.

It was, of course, impossible to control food supplies so that everyone received exactly the same amount of food. Lord Woolton, the Minister of Food, made no pretence that this was his intention. His job, he said, was to see to it that everyone received the minimum amount of protein and vitamins necessary to ensure good health under hard working conditions. He was not running the Ministry of Food to prevent people from obtaining extra food if they could legitimately do so.

Between January 1940, when rationing was introduced, and the following April, when Lord Woolton became Minister of Food, only five items had been rationed. Bacon, ham and butter were rationed to 4 ounces per head per week, sugar to 12 ounces. Everyone over 6 years old was allowed 1s. 10d.-worth of meat per week; under 6 the allowance was 11d. As the war progressed more and more foodstuffs were rationed. To obtain rations, coupons from the ration book issued to every individual had to be surrendered to the retailer from whom the food was bought. Later a points rationing scheme was introduced, to supplement coupon rations. Under the points scheme items of food, generally tinned or dried goods, were given a value of so many points, and each ration-book holder was permitted to purchase whatever goods they liked up to a maximum periodic points allowance. The 'points' value of a commodity could be varied according to the supply situation. If the item were plentiful, the points value was lowered so that stocks could be sold more easily. If it were scarce, the points value would be raised thus reducing demand.

Some goods, bread and vegetables, were not rationed, but distributed under a system known as Controlled Distribution. Every household in the country was encouraged, in the 'Dig for Victory' campaign, to produce some vegetables of their own, wherever they could find a patch of ground. Much more agricultural land than before the war was given over to the production of vegetables. Even so, some supplies, such as onions, became very scarce. A chief source of the supply of onions and tomatoes had been the Channel Islands, and the cargoes of these vegetables coming into Britain came to an abrupt end when the Channel Islands were occupied by German troops in June 1940. When there were not enough vegetables to be distributed to all areas of the country, supplies were allocated to one area only. If the shortage remained acute the supply was directed to another area after a period of a few weeks so that the hardship of doing without should be fairly equitably shared.

At the Ministry of Food, Lord Woolton was well aware of the value of good publicity. It was his task to make a shift in the national diet away from foods which had to be imported towards those which could more easily be produced at home. The most important home-produced staple food was the potato, both for its nutritional qualities and for its relative ease of cultivation. Through press advertisements, *Food Flashes* on the wireless and on the cinema screen, the cartoon characters of 'Potato Pete' and his compatriot 'Dr Carrot' became universally known. The success of the campaign was undeniable, as the consumption of vegetables, and potatoes and carrots in particular, rose enormously.

The shift in diet was helped by the fact that a large proportion of the population was able to buy fresh vegetables frequently for the first time. For many years before the war, wages had been so low, the price of vegetables high, and the knowledge of their nutritional value limited to a tiny section of the population, that many people just did not eat them. The intensive publicity and the raising of many families' income to decent subsistence levels meant a high rate of increase in consumption, which Britain's farmers were hard put to keep up with.

The change of diet was most marked in the poorest city areas: the corresponding improvement in the state of health of that part of the population gave cause for much satisfaction on the part of the Ministry of Food.

" Once upon a time there was a princess who lived in a garden full of rows and rows and rows of lovely onions . . ."

In the countryside, fresh vegetables had always and obviously been more widely eaten and more freely available. Few farmers, farmworkers, and their families needed to be encouraged to dig a vegetable patch for victory. The reaction of most of the evacuated families coming into country families from the poorer districts of the cities was that people in the countryside ate enormously well, and this was before some of the staple foods of a poorer urban diet (fish, to go with chips, jam, to spread on bread) had become difficult to obtain. In consequence, rationing probably impinged less on families living in the countryside, since they were more used to the sort of diet that was being officially encouraged, and they were closer to the source of supply.

One of the principal commodities available in the agricultural areas which aroused particular envy amongst city dwellers was eggs. When supplies were at their lowest, families in the towns were rationed to one egg per person per fortnight. There were few farms which did not have a collection of hens and the sight of fresh eggs every morning gladdened the eyes of

January 1940 saw the introduction of rationing *right* and increasing publicity to urge people to conserve and utilise their food supplies to the last ounce.

Milling rose hips *below* in an ice-cream factory. The rose hips were collected largely by children to overcome a national shortage of vitamins.

Marauders, American medium bombers, *above* parked on a bare English heath. *Right* Agricultural land disappearing beneath the new concrete runways being prepared for a US bomber station.

every holidaymaker, worker or billeted serviceman who normally suffered the stinginess of the urban diet.

Rationing food was bound to create something of a black market and it was a remarkable feature of the food supply situation in the Second World War that this was kept, through strict policing, to a minimum of activity, or at least a minimum of publicity. To some extent, however, it did operate and the easier supply of money, created by higher industrial earnings, lubricated its mechanism. In the countryside, the restrictions of wartime were capable of more flexible solutions. The farther away from London or urban administrative centres the more malleable seemed the rules. Although it was illegal to traffic in foodstuffs, a system of barter developed in a quiet way in a number of places, under which a surplus of vegetables might be traded for a few cans of precious petrol from a local garage. A cow might suddenly injure itself, and have to be killed and the carcass divided up in order not to waste the meat, in return for some extra flour for bread-making, a new tractor tyre, a rare bottle of spirits, with perhaps some English cigarettes. In spite of the influx of new faces into the countryside, unaccounted-for strangers, who might be looking into these matters, were very rare,

American medical orderlies prescribe a ration of chewing gum for the children of an East Anglian village.

and could be spotted with little difficulty. Farmyards, outhouses, concealing hedges and crooked ditches offered more opportunity for interesting evidence to disappear than did small backyards and the squat, square bareness of suspected city streets.

Even the comparative plenty of fresh foods in the countryside was as nothing compared with the fantastic stores of foodstuffs brought to Britain by Allied shipping to feed the thousands of US army soldiers and airmen who were stationed in the southern and eastern counties. From 1942 onwards there was a continuous increase in the number of American troops, preparing for an Allied invasion of Europe. Camps were thrown up and new airfields built, all of which added to the strain on the diminishing stock of agricultural land. A number of country houses were taken over and pressed into service as operations headquarters, or officers' accommodation.

The rations provided for American troops by the US Government were far in excess of those provided for the British Army and in a different world from the food available to the British civilian. Dances and Christmas parties thrown by the American army provided fairy-tale quantities of ice-cream, cakes, chocolate and buns as well as endless supplies of a drink virtually unobtainable in wartime Britain – fresh coffee. Despite initial wariness and a few incidents in which national sensibilities were offended, the Americans came to be accepted and welcomed by the British people. Their largesse – fruit and sweets for the children, cigarettes for men and women, silk stockings for their girl-friends – obviously helped, but the variety and gusto which they brought to the life of many a small country town, as well as to the city centres, often provided a welcome element of cheer and optimism in the hard, austere days of restricted and rationed wartime life.

An American camp was a source of delight to local girls and, no doubt, vice versa. British boy-friends had to struggle against a barrage of riches, goodies, candies and the novelty of a foreign yet familiar approach to life, which approximated at least to the image of it portrayed on the cinema screen. Perhaps the people who enjoyed the Americans' presence most of all were the children. It seemed that few American soldiers could pass a group of children without doling out sweets, chocolate or chewing gum. Although many mothers strictly forbade their children to ask for sweets, a greeting or a smile was often all that was necessary to open the Americans' treasure-chest. Christmas parties also provided the opportunity for exciting rides in the ubiquitous jeeps in which the Americans motored about the countryside.

Petrol-rationing meant that military vehicles virtually had the roads to themselves. In the gradual build-up to D-Day, many of the roads in the southern counties of England were turned into one-way military convoy routes. Army lorries and wide American staff cars encountered endless problems in negotiating the narrow country lanes. As preparations for the invasion advanced, the southern counties were slowly turned into a huge military vehicle and equipment store. The new Winchester by-pass, completed just before war broke out, was not opened to civilian traffic but was used to park mile upon mile of military transport and armoured vehicles, ready to be moved to Southampton when the invasion began.

On the other side of the hedgerows, harvest-time brought an increased throb and clatter of new machinery with every passing year of the war. In 1942, more than a thousand combine harvesters enabled an enormous harvest of grain, culled from $8\frac{1}{2}$ million acres of ground, to be gathered in. The rate of production of threshed grain from so much machinery caused problems farther down the line. Almost as much time and labour had to be expended in getting the grain into sacks, transporting it and drying it before it went to be milled as had been saved by the machinery in the harvest fields themselves. In the fields, too, the distant war in the Far East made itself felt. The many imported binding machines used a twine made of hemp, the main supplies of which came from the Philippines. Once overrun by the Japanese, the Philippines no longer exported the hemp and all reserve stocks were used in the harvest of 1942.

Although the weather at harvest-time was unsettled, and farmers in the west of England were bedevilled by rain, the summer had again been long and hot, and the crops had ripened well. The ground itself was in good shape, since the curiously repetitive wartime pattern of severely frosty winters and generally dry springs had broken down heavy clay soils which had previously borne only poor crops of grass before the war and turned them into highly cultivable land. The results were evident at this harvest, for yields were extremely high throughout the whole range of agricultural produce. The targets for the production of potatoes and sugar-beet were easily surpassed. The good fortune of the farmers was the saving of the nation's food supplies. Shipping losses were heavy, and the tonnage of meat, fats, eggs, fruit and sugar coming into the country was very low indeed. Britain's agricultural production made up for most of the losses, not by supplying the same foodstuffs, but by growing the raw materials for substantial and nutritious filling foods.

Two of 1942's efforts never really caught on. The National Loaf, introduced in an attempt to eke out still further the supplies of wheat, was made from a

D-Day *below* Sherman tanks of the US Army exercising on Salisbury Plain, preparatory to leaving England for Europe. *Right* British infantrymen mounting a mock assault on a cliff-top in southern England. *Bottom* GIs resting before taking ship for the Normandy beaches and the invasion of Europe.

grey, wholemeal flour which produced a dark, coarse bread. It was not popular and many minor digestive illnesses were blamed onto the National Loaf. The Ministry supplied the housewives battling on the 'Kitchen Front' with ammunition in the form of recipes which used only ingredients which were reasonably freely available. The epitome of these, Woolton Pie, was, however, generally considered to be one of the most unpleasant dishes of the war. It contained a mixture of carrots, parsnips, turnips and potatoes, covered in a thick, white sauce, to give it added moisture, and baked in a pastry case. It emerged in colour, taste and consistency as an unappetising, stodgy pie and many people were surprised that Lord Woolton, one of the most popular of the wartime ministers, who had an accurate sense of public opinions and desires, should have put his name to it.

Compared with pre-war farming, work on the land, particularly in arable farming, was being created and performed at a tremendous pace. Wages had risen, workers had been diverted back to the land, the volunteers of the WLA gave added assistance and mechanisation had increased output enormously particularly during the weeks at harvest time. The weather, kind to the farmers for five war years in succession, had played an incalculable part in ensuring the success of the increased production. By 1943, it looked as though the peak had been reached. Another dry spring and long, hot weeks in June and July meant that a good harvest was again in prospect, and could begin early. Most of the beet and potatoes and the large East Anglian corn harvest was gathered in successfully, the load of labour on the backs of both men and machines having been spread over a usefully long period of warm weather. But in western and northern districts the good fortune at last deserted the farmers. The clouds and rain rolled in from the Atlantic during August and stayed put for the autumn. Sheaves of corn which had been stooked in the early days of August were still standing uncollected in the water-logged fields in October. Heavy rain made potato-picking a sodden, arduous task as the soaking, muddy ground yielded up with difficulty a damaged crop. Much of the corn crop was lost completely, a serious blow to the production targets, and a financial loss to both farmers and the Government, who provided cash subsidies and supplies of fertiliser.

The heavy loss of crops through bad weather at harvest time was a risk that had to be taken if British agriculture were to bridge the gap between the needs of the population and the loss of imports through restrictions on and damage to shipping. The experience of 1943 led many farmers and other agricultural experts to advise a reduction in the cropping programme for 1944, partly to reduce the risk of another widespread loss of crops, but perhaps more importantly because

A V-1 flying bomb, caught by the cable attached to the barrage balloon, crashed onto the nearby barn.

some of the land intensively cropped badly needed a fallow year, or a year under temporary grass, in order to regain its fertility. Taking stock of the situation at the end of 1943 revealed other difficulties for the year ahead. There were serious shortages in the supplies of basic equipment due to its intensive use in previous years and the obstacles in the way of repair and replacement. New sources of fertiliser were always a problem. But by 1944 stocks of such items as binder twine, milk churns, sacks for potatoes and grain and other unglamorous but essential equipment were heavily depleted. The supply of heavier machinery, which in early years had been imported from the United States, had diminished as American factories built up their production of arms and military equipment, and much of the farm machinery that was produced was used to re-equip and supplement the machinery already in use on the north American continent.

New problems beset the potato growers. Not only did the harvesting of potatoes have to wait until the huge grain harvest was gathered in, but they in their turn delayed the picking of other root crops and the sugar beet. Disease too, had begun to spread in the most intensively-cropped areas. Eelworm attacked the

A Kentish oasthouse reduced to a ruin after being hit by a flying bomb in 1944.

potato crop and the only means of destroying it was to stop growing potatoes.

Despite advice and the increasing difficulties, the Government decided to maintain agricultural production at the peak level of 1943. The decision was influenced by the fact that shipping space would probably be reduced still further by the imminent, although by no means certain, invasion of Europe. Once the invasion had taken place, and assuming that the Germans were driven back towards Germany, the peoples of Europe, who had been living under conditions of food supply very much worse than the population of Britain, would also need feeding. Some of the food at least would have to come from the fields of Britain.

When the weather allowed, in the winter months of 1943, the farmers prepared their land for yet another colossal effort at food production. The crops were rotated around the available fields. There was hardly any extra land to be ploughed, and that which was available would only deliver poor yields. A balance was struck between the projected crops of barley, oats and wheat, so that more oats should be available as fodder for cattle, in order that the milk yield should not suffer. This was gained by relaxing a directive which

had caused some of the oat crop to be directed to the maltsters for the brewing of beer to make up for the loss of a portion of their barley which had been used to supplement wheat in the flour for breadmaking.

In June 1944, the long-awaited attack on Fortress Europe began, and the huge invading army which had turned the whole of the south of England, including much of its agricultural land, into an army camp set sail for the beaches of Normandy. The weather, fair for invasion, promised great things for the equally historic occupation of harvesting the crops. It lasted long enough for the warriors to gain their first objective, the beachhead in France. Their compatriots in the fields were less lucky. In 1944, not only the western and northern districts, but the whole country suffered heavy rain in August and September and wet gales sweeping in with the autumn made harvesting almost 11 million acres of corn and root crops an exhausting, frustrating and infuriating task. Farmers in the southeast of England had to contend with the further imposition of attack by flying bombs and rockets. In spite of it all, the final tally of crops harvested was only slightly below the level of 1943. The farmers' struggle had been as fierce, in many ways, as that of the contending armies; their achievement in providing the fuel for the human energy which created the output of supplies for the invading armies was as successful as the progress of the armies themselves.

Victory and After

Although no-one could be certain, everyone desperately hoped that the farmers' year which began once the harvest of 1944 was gathered in would see out the Second World War. Many of the fields had been cropped almost into infertility; there was just enough land to spare to graze the dairy herds upon which the nation's milk supply, vital to its health, depended; machinery needed to be overhauled and buildings needed repair and replacement. As in every other walk of life in Britain, by Christmas 1944 the talk was of what would happen after the war, when the pressures had changed. In the farming industry the question most often took the form of speculation as to the future relationship between the farmers and the Government. The crisis of war had brought the two parties together into an enforced co-operation which had achieved remarkable results. Would the co-operation continue once the enemy's threats to the shipping routes bringing food into Britain had been silenced? Countless words were spoken and written during the last years of the war about the bright future that agriculture should have in post-war Britain. But any farmer over forty could remember the same tune being played after the First World War, and the sorry plight in which the farming community found itself not many years afterwards.

Prospects looked different from the various regions of the countryside. The intensive nature of wartime farming had in many ways emphasised the variety of British agriculture. Although the overall picture was one of mixed farming with a high proportion of cereal crops, it was obviously most efficient, in the individual areas, to grow the crops which best suited the local conditions of soil, topography and climate. Some farmers feared more than others for the future of the style of farming into which they had been directed by an omnipotent Government, which might be succeeded by a peacetime government with very different views on the role of agriculture in the nation's life.

These worries were in the backs of the minds of the farmers of East Anglia. Before the war, their farming, principally of cereal crops and sugar-beet, had been aided by the Government through parliamentary regulation of the price of wheat and a subsidy for the production of sugar-beet. The war had seen immense activity in these products. Pigs and sheep that had been kept had been gradually sold off; pastures had been ploughed up and much money invested in new machinery, particularly in combine harvesters. The farmers were able to expand production in this way through the increasing level of demand which the wartime Government had ordained. It was essential to their future prosperity that such demand be maintained.

Arable farmers in Scotland had managed to pursue a more general course of farming. A shortage of milk and good prices for dairy products meant that the number of cows kept on Scottish farms, where grazing was good, increased over the war years. This trend occurred in spite of extra cropping which reduced the amount of permanent or temporary grasslands. With the high demand for potatoes, which were grown intensively in Scotland, likely to continue after the war during the years when the hopefully liberated European nations would need to be fed from Allied resources, the farmers of the Scottish lowlands seemed to be well situated to meet peacetime conditions.

The real revolution in British farming had occurred in those areas which before the war had been involved almost exclusively in dairy farming. In 1939, 80 per cent of the land in a broad belt across the English midlands was under pasture. Of the rest, quite a high proportion was given over to market gardening, with only a few fields of cereal or root crops interspersed among the herds of cattle and sheep. The revolution was not only in the use of land. To plough it up and turn over to arable farming, as the Government

A cheery wave salutes the achievement of the farmers' task – feeding the nation at war.

Entire villages were evacuated in order that troops could practise assault landings in preparation for D-Day. In Devon, three thousand people had to move from their homes for an unspecified time at six weeks' notice.

ordained, meant a desperate search for more staff and the purchase or building of homes for them to live in. The Midlands had for so many years been a dairying region, that it was difficult to find enough men who had any experience of using a plough or planting corn at all. It also took 2 years of increasing arable farming to get a crop rotation system successfully established. During that 2 years the diminishing area of grassland and the lack of by-products from the establishing crop-rotation farming meant that foodstuff for the large numbers of cattle held on the farm was in very short supply. Once the system was established, the Midlands was transformed into a region of healthy mixed farming, worked by labour, machinery and limitless advice and instruction supplied by the War Agricultural Committees. The problem which the peace was likely to bring was one of finding enough people to continue to work the land in its new guise.

Throughout the war years, the farmer short of hands at harvest time, or about to embark on some major project to take in new land, had only to telephone the local War Agricultural Committee's offices and a gang of Women's Land Army volunteers or other mobile workers would usually be directed to assist him for as long as they were needed. It made for good production levels on the farms, but a high incidence of low productivity, since it was easy to cover weak organisation of farm workers by drafting in extra helpers whenever they became necessary. When farms were working flat out, from the winter of 1942 onwards, the supply of WLA volunteers was obviously limited, since the vast proportion of the entire British working population had been mobilised into some form of work connected with the war effort. Nevertheless, help was available through obvious channels, whereas after the war the farms would have to be kept running on labour attracted by good working and living conditions, and high and stable wage rates.

In the hillier areas of the western and northern districts of the kingdom, mixed farming, with a high proportion of livestock, including pigs and poultry, had been the general rule before the war. The shortage of foodstuffs and the emphasis on arable farming had a particularly serious effect on these more specialised

The gunner *above* shot down a V-1 flying bomb at 300 yards' range, which promptly crashed into his comrades-in-arms' living quarters, seen devastated in the background.

The old gentleman *below* avoided the devastation which killed his family because he had been taking his dog for a walk before his Sunday lunch.

farms. Farmers who had fertile lowland pastures within their boundaries were better able to adjust the balance of their activities and their income than those who farmed higher up the hillsides and on the moorlands. These men faced some of the most intractable problems presented by the demands of wartime agriculture – poor soil, steep fields, lack of machinery and implements for arable farming and loss of output from their livestock. Any post-war national agricultural policy would have to give a clear indication of whether they were expected to build up their holdings of pigs and poultry once more or receive some definite and permanent assistance from the state, since their farms were only marginally profitable under wartime conditions.

The greatest single revolutionary feature of British agriculture brought about by the crisis of war was the vast and rapid increase in mechanisation. The number of tractors in use in 1939, about 15,000, had almost trebled by the end of the war. Their use saved many

hours of work and much expense in the way of wages and daily attendance and feeding of horses. Because of the speed and endurance of a tractor, farm work could be done when weather conditions were favourable, and consequently far more efficiently than when ploughs, for instance, were drawn by horses who could cover a smaller area per hour and were limited to a shorter working day.

To get the best use out of it, the tractor had to be selected from a number of various types, according to the land it was going to work. Although a larger machine could pull a wider plough which created more furrows per traverse of a field, many British farms were not designed for large-scale operation, and smaller power-units were found to be much more appropriate. The fields had evolved to the scale of horse operations: many farms were described as one-team, two-team farms, and so on. Some agricultural visionaries foresaw the day when farms would be co-operative ventures, and large-scale mechanised ploughing and harvesting would be made possible by the opening out of the fields. Many more farmers, concerned with making a daily living, bought smaller tractors which were suitable for their own individual scale of opera-

tions. As tractors became more widely used, it was discovered that a number of smaller tractors were of more use and could be employed more efficiently than a large one, especially at harvest time when there were a lot of short frequent journeys to be made between the fields and the ricks.

Tractors were simply the motive power. Throughout the war new and improved agricultural implements were constantly tried, tested, adapted and built or bought from the United States. Cultivators and harrows for preparing the soil before planting were all newly-developed for use with motorised power. One of the principal differences in the operation of the new implements was that the man doing the job was up ahead of the work, sitting on the tractor, rather than behind, following the horses. This meant the introduction of various refinements to farm implements such as harrows or drags which were used to clear the soil of weeds or old grass. The horse-harrow could be cleared of its accumulated unwanted vegetation by the carter simply lifting the corner of the harrow and proceeding on his way. The mechanised version had to be self-clearing, if the tractor-driver was not to interrupt his operation every time the harrow became clogged.

New forms of seed drill were introduced, which not only planted seed, but laid a circle of artificial manure around each seed. This was much more economical

Threshing by steam power – a widespread practice during wartime due to the diminished petrol supplies for other forms of engine.

The farmer's problems were not removed by a victorious war, nor did technological progress alter the basic tasks or men's reliance on their traditional solutions.

than the old practice of broadcasting manure, in the hope that a good proportion of it would find its way through the soil to nourish the seed. Binders and hay-making machinery were all added to the farmers' common armoury of implements, but the single item, after the tractor, which attracted most attention and effort in its development was the combine harvester. Originally built for use on the prairies of the North American continent, it combined the jobs of stooking corn, of carting it, ricking, thatching and threshing, all in the one operation. The drastically-reduced labour costs soon made combine harvesters, particularly self-propelling versions (the first were hauled by tractors) indispensable on the large corn-growing farms of the eastern counties of England.

In some areas of the country where rainfall was higher than in the east, the threshing machine was not replaced by the combine harvester, because corn had often to be harvested in a half-wet condition, in which state it could not go straight through a combine harvester to be threshed. It had to be stored, often for some weeks, in a rick or bin, and threshed after it had dried out. Threshing-machines did not change much

in design, although the war brought necessary improvements in details such as bearings and rubber tyres (when the rubber was available), which made them easier to move about in wet weather than on the old wooden or metal-rimmed wheels. A number were driven by internal combustion engines but, since petrol was comparatively expensive and scarce during the war, many were worked by steam engines, which had performed valiant service over many tens of years.

Many other mechanised implements were introduced to or developed for British wartime farming. During the war years more than £100 million was spent on mechanising British agriculture. Since the pre-war market for farm machinery had been so small, there was no manufacturing industry ready to meet such demand, so almost the entire sum was spent abroad. It was forecast that when the war ended a great deal of the machinery used continuously during the war would have to be replaced. The opportunity for an agricultural implement industry was going to be immense – if the farmers had the capital available to invest in new machinery. The opportunity for farming to flourish through efficient use of machines and for industry to grow supplying that machinery depended, as did ultimately all questions of the farmers' future, upon the attitude the post-war Government was going to take towards the status of farming.

Two German generals and an admiral harvesting oats. Even after the war in Europe had ended, prisoners-of-war were not immediately repatriated.

School children helping with the potato harvest at Bilton, Yorkshire. School parties were organised to ease the shortage of farm labour.

The wartime Government was, of course, beset with conflicting advice about what policy to adopt towards British agriculture once the war was over. As in other matters it declined to make any detailed pronouncements. Winston Churchill's policy was simply to win the war, and for most of it he avoided giving any indication of the particular sort of society he wished to see emerge once peace was won. The pre-war conflict over the role of the British country-side between the one faction who believed it should be a leisure-ground for an industrial society fed by food imported from abroad, and another who believed that agricultural small-holdings should form the basis of a new British society with individual farming at its heart, was complicated by the rapid mechanisation of the industry. In 1939, few in the farming community foresaw the day when combine harvesters cutting their swathes across large, open fields, producing threshed grain at the end of the day, would be the rule rather than the exception.

The proponents of rural reconstruction, the romantic, back-to-the-land movement, envisaged their society as a multiplication of the numbers of people engaged in fairly small farming operations as many

were in the 1930s. Their ideas were severely castigated by those who agreed that Britain's agriculture was due for a renaissance, but argued, far more convincingly, that it should be based on a scientific application of technological developments, not only in the field of farm machinery, but in the breeding of crops and livestock and in manures and foodstuffs to nourish them. There were some extremists who took the arguments for mechanics too far; the more sensible minds recognised the everlasting need for those who worked on the land to have a sense of care and skill based on practice and experience gained in years on the job. No dairy herd could hope to produce its best yields without the ministrations of a first class stockman who knew his cattle literally inside out. But that stockman should also be able to run a mechanised dairy, and maintain it to the highest standards of cleanliness and hygiene required to produce high-quality milk, free from bacteria.

The need for the retention of traditional skills did not mean that Britain's agriculture should be re-directed towards an industry of yeomen farmers and peasant smallholders. Rural crafts already becoming fashionably patronised by preservers of the picturesque

The future of farming was already a subject for propaganda, whilst women were still being asked to volunteer for the WLA.

were no substitute for sound technical knowledge of modern farm implements and practices. The idyllic world of bucolic tranquility was a myth idealised mostly by those who lived in towns. In the post-war international world, in which the prairies of the United States and Canada would be offering their wares in the same world marketplace as British farmers, economic survival would be won only by the societies who ran their industries and provided for their food stores in the most efficient way. The way ahead for British farming lay in the rationalisation of the corn-producing areas into units capable of extensive use of combine harvesters and a general shift towards a smaller, more highly-skilled and better-trained body of farm workers than existed before the war. Such men could only be encouraged to enter or to remain in farming if the conditions were good, if wages were reasonable, if housing was satisfactory, and if the attractions of industrial and urban life did not outweigh the benefits agricultural employment had to offer.

Although there was obviously going to be no definite lead from Churchill's wartime coalition Government on the post-war status of agriculture, the debate ranged over the duties a government might be expected to undertake. If the romanticists had their way, the state would have to subsidise the rural peasant economy for the dwellers in the countryside to maintain any reasonable level of subsistence. The more general conclusion was that a government's part should be to avoid subsidy, but to regulate production so that booms and slumps which would distort the price level of agricultural produce could be smoothed out as much as possible. Guaranteed prices and guaranteed markets were a common feature of most agricultural economic proposals. It was also widely agreed that the balance of post-war farming should be different from that of the inter-war years. Larger-scale corn production and higher milk yields from livestock farming were going to be 2 important requisites of the British population as a whole. Whether the establishment and maintenance of land-use levels should be engineered through the authority of the War Agricultural Committees in a peacetime guise, and whether market conditions should be allowed to prevail and adjust the balance under the control of marketing boards for individual agricultural products, as they had done before the war, were matters for more intense discussion as the war appeared to be moving into its final phase.

In the last resort, the discussion was more concerned with means than with principles. It was largely agreed that *laissez-faire* in agriculture was dead. The combination of the speed of modern transport and the accessibility of markets all over the world made some form of control necessary, if adverse world trading conditions were not to impinge too severely on the farming communities of any one country. Market stability and a benignly controlled freedom were ideals which extended beyond the individual farmer and his local market town, to the inter-regional, national scene and to relations between nation states. Stability was vital for prosperity and organised planning, which alone could lead to efficient industry. Control was necessary to prevent poor-quality goods, or contaminated, bacteria-ridden produce from reaching the market place and being sold for the same return as good produce.

It was hoped that international market stability might be gained by the greater involvement of national buying bodies in the world market places. The culprits of the pre-war fluctuation in price, and the consequent distress and insecurity of the farming community, were seen to be the nation states which sold produce in bulk, and the individual merchants, the middle-men, who bought it. The fact that nations were in the market-place as sellers, but only rarely as buying bodies, produced a chronic instability in the trade in agricultural produce. The pre-war French Government, for instance, subsidised its wheat farmers to the extent

A hay loader being demonstrated towards the end of the war. Piles of mown hay were scooped up and mechanically pushed up the loader into a wagon.

that they received the equivalent of sixty shillings a quarter. French wheat could be bought in Bristol for eighteen shillings a quarter, a price far below the cost of production. Because of the French Government's subsidy, wheat was available in Britain at a very much lower price than that at which British farmers were able to produce it. Merchants importing the cheap wheat who, when criticised, claimed that they were serving the community by enabling it to buy cheap food, were at the same time doing a serious disservice to the agricultural section of the community by making arable farming completely uneconomic.

A solution was seen to lie in persuading governments that buying on a national scale, with the nation's interests at heart, rather than those of the individual entrepeneur, was the best way of regulating the movement of international trade to the advantage of both producer and consumer. Numerous mechanisms were proposed through which this might be done. One of the most serious was the proposal for the constitution of a National Import Board, which would act as an umbrella organisation for national boards dealing with individual agricultural commodities. Their function being to fix prices and production levels, to improve quality and to facilitate distribution, such proposed boards were the direct descendents of the Milk Marketing Board, the Bacon Marketing Board, the Hop Marketing Board and others which had existed before the war. The principal difference in the post-war version was to be the composition of the personnel of these boards. Producers, retailers and consumers

Self-propelled hoe for hoeing 'row crops', an improvement over tractor-drawn hoes since the operator could examine closely the work being done.

should all be represented, so that the producer's prices, the retailer's costs and the level of consumer demand should all be reflected in the final prices agreed upon.

Before the war, the boards were entirely in the hands of the industries they served. Producers and manufacturers had powerful voices and were often less interested in progress towards better products and more efficient industry than they were in maintaining their own level of profits. Price levels were often fixed so that the least efficient farmer could still cover his costs and make a profit. This meant that the efficient farmers made a great deal more profit, the distributors and retailers added their margin and the price to the consumer ended at a very high level. Under uncontrolled market conditions, the reduced costs of efficient farming would be reflected in a lower price for the goods, so that the market price would fall below the inefficient farmer's cost of production, thus causing him to lose money. The pre-war marketing boards enabled the efficient farmer to exist, at the cost of prices to the consumer which were prohibitively high to large numbers of the population. It was hoped that the proposed post-war boards would take a much more equitable view of all sides of the industry, from producer to consumer.

The activities of the individual marketing boards would of necessity be restricted by the overall policy of the proposed National Import Board. The policy would be informed by a judicious review of what was available from the production of British farms and what was available on the world markets to make up for the difference between Britain's needs and its own produce. In particular, the National Board should be aware of surpluses and refuse to buy in from abroad a crop such as maize, for cattle feed, which cannot be grown in Britain because of the climate, if there were a surplus of oats in the country which could be used for the same purpose. Bran, a high-quality cattle-feed made as a by-product of milling wheat into flour should be brought in by buying the wheat and milling it in Britain, rather than buying bran milled abroad.

Such were the directions in which the international boards were supposed to move. For the system to be of any avail, some form of co-ordination and control was needed at local level. It was obvious that in peacetime the organisation of the War Agricultural Committees would no longer be tenable. To begin with, they were appointed from above, rather than elected by those with whom they had to deal. Once empowered, the members of the War Agricultural Committees could only be removed by a decision from the Ministry of Agriculture. If the acts or directives of the Committee members were disliked or objected to by farmers, there was nothing that could be done about it. The War Agricultural Committee's decision was final and allowed of no appeal. From the other side of the fence, most of the members of War Agricultural Committees were

Summer 1944 on the beach at Lowestoft. Although the danger of invasion had passed, beach defences were still in position.

unlikely to agree to serve on any similar body if it were to be set up in peacetime. For the duration of the crisis of war they were prepared to serve in the national interest, but it was foreign to the nature of many men to be placed in a position of indisputable authority over their equals, without the approval of their colleagues through the process of election.

One of the most difficult problems to be faced, whatever the means of local administration adopted, was that of the farmer who farmed badly. During the war he was evicted, and someone else took over the farm. Before the war a landlord whose tenant was farming badly had to compensate that tenant if he were asked to leave the farm. Such pressure could, in any case, only be applied if a committee of local farmers agreed that a tenant farmer was farming so badly that he should be forced to leave the land, and it was rare that a man's neighbours would judge that he deserved to be evicted. A bad farmer who owned his land was,

of course, simply a liability on the land about which there was nothing to be done.

In a way, a feeling deeply felt but probably not frequently expressed, that the war was being fought to uphold and preserve certain fundamental standards of freedom and security, was the parent of the idea that after the war such sittings in judgement and summary evictions should be a thing of the past. The criterion should simply be one of business efficiency, where efficiency indicated not only high productivity, but high-quality production. Prices for good and poor produce should be adjusted so that the inefficient farmer either improved his output or ceased to farm.

On many farms, efficiency was hindered by the size of the holding, and, often, the scattering of the fields. The farms were designed for working by horse and ox-teams. Farms, divided for generations between the heirs to the land, were often separated into plots which did not adjoin each other. Rationalisation, under the guidance of a local agricultural authority, should take the form of reapportioning the land of farmers whose owners died or retired so that it would become part of the holding onto which it adjoined.

116

Many saw in these ideas the spectre or the banner, depending on their traditions and current political views, of the nationalisation of land. Overall, the view tended to be against nationalisation. Arguments which have a familiar ring today were thrown up – that if the nation owned the land it could not afford to farm it at a loss. In response, people pointed to the example of Eire, where much of the land was owned by the state, and before the war there had been a great deal more dereliction of the land than had been the case on the farmland of Great Britain. Also the fact was that the County Councils of Britain owned a good deal of farmland anyway. Being able to borrow money at the cheapest rates, call on government financial assistance and find the money to offset deficits from public funds had not led to conspicuously better farming on publicly-owned land.

Amongst all the other problems, the coming of peace would bring with it the difficulties of a return to civilian life of a vast number of men and women who had served in the Forces and earned their living defending the nation. When the country no longer needed defending in quite such an active manner, many hundreds of thousands of men and women would be looking for a new way to provide for themselves and their families. The vocal elements in the agricultural world were quick to point out that the work they had carried out during the war had been done often with the minimum of manpower, and much of it had been

Margate promenade being cleared of its barbed wire by a detachment of ARP workers.

available only on a temporary basis through institutions such as the Women's Land Army. If agriculture were to pursue the vigorous course which they hoped a peacetime government would choose for it, then its needs for manpower would be great.

In order to attract men and women being demobilised, working on the land had to be made to seem worthwhile. Although general wartime government comment had indicated that the future of agriculture would be far more prosperous than its recent past, no specific promises had been made. Remembering the years immediately following the First World War, no farmer would have put faith in them anyway. Nevertheless efforts were made, for the sake of those already in the industry, and for those who might enter it, to keep the approximate parity in basic wage rates between agricultural and urban industrial employment. In February 1945, the minimum wage for a farm worker was fixed at £3 10s. for a forty-eight hour week.

Better conditions as well as higher wages had also to be borne in mind. Whilst the war was still in progress the Government promised to build 3,000 new cottages to improve housing conditions for agricultural workers which were often miserably poor. A number of farmers or farm workers who examined or lived in the new cottages felt that a great chance had been missed in the design of these cottages, which were on very traditional lines. They argued, along with planners of new post-war towns, that there should be much more experiment in the layout and fittings of new houses. Such experiments, to see whether they would be the living conditions of the future, involved the installation of electric

Victory *below* celebrated in the Channel Islands,
right spelt out by the tables of a children's street party,
far right symbolised by the parades, held throughout the
country, of the services and war workers. *Bottom* the
popular Americans say a traditional farewell to their
English village home.

cookers instead of the old coal-fired kitchen range, radiators for heating, airing cupboards for drying clothes, bathrooms and indoor sanitation. The most curious also wanted to know whether refrigerators could be used economically, or whether they were, in fact, necessary at all.

With discussion of the nature of the new housing went arguments about its status. The fiercest debate was over the question of tied cottages. It was an anciently-established agricultural industry practice which provided a cottage to go with a farm-worker's job, often at a very low rent. The Agricultural Workers Union had for some years before the war been agitating against the practice, and when there was some indication that a whole new deal for agriculture might be in the offing once the war was won, the Union increased the urgency of its argument. Their fear was a repetition of a number of instances in which farmers had abused their responsibility in providing accommodation. If there were little alternative housing in the district, the worker living in a tied cottage was forced to remain with the farmer for whom he worked, since if he chose to leave, he and his family would be without a home. With this lever of pressure, an unscrupulous farmer was able to hold down the wages of his workers.

Although the abuses of the system were recognised, many farmers, tenants as well as landlords, felt that the tied cottage system had a value, if properly used, in attracting good workers to a farm. It was realised that the houses would have to be of a high standard in the future, probably new, certainly with none of the disadvantages of a partially-converted Victorian rural slum. Skilled farm workers such as stockmen were earning up to £5 a week, and would not be prepared to live in anything less than their status and income entitled them to.

Such men were virtually certain of stable employment and reasonable conditions for 3 or 4 years after the end of the war at least. For the army of volunteers, many of whom wished to stay on the land, or the ex-Service personnel, the times were less sure. The women of the WLA were almost certain to be ousted from their jobs, if they were hoping to stay in them, by men returning from the wars. Hopeful schemes for government-sponsored smallholdings were proposed but moved little farther than the drawing-board.

Such smallholdings were part of a notion that was much discussed in various contexts and derived from the ideals of a green, peaceful, rural England which had lain in the back of many people's minds, even a number of those from the cities, when they had decided or been ordered to fight or work for King and Country. It manifested itself in schemes for setting up small poultry farms to be run by men demobbed from the Forces, or putting up a capital loan for them to begin small concerns of this sort. Such ideas were in one

New housing *top* to shelter the many families whose houses had been destroyed or damaged. *Above* the old and the new, a century between them.

sense complementary to the internationalism of the schemes for stable agricultural market through economic co-operation between the nations. Smallholdings in the field of market-gardening, fruit-growing or poultry farming were the tiniest atomic units of the universe of global agricultural organisation. In another sense, however, they were inward-looking ideas, the beginnings of a desire to escape from the frightening scale that the Second World War had assumed. They were schemes close to the dreams of the rural reconstructionists who mistakenly envisaged the village economy as the basis of the nation's future prosperity.

Kentish farm workers subjected to squalid living conditions even after the end of the war. Such conditions were a powerful advertisement for housing renewal.

And they were ideal situations based on the premise that the co-operation which flowed through a Britain mobilised by wartime regulations and sharing the common burden of fierce attack from an external enemy would continue when that threat had ceased.

It was widely acknowledged that the pre-war constitution of British society, with its glaring ills and inequalities, would not, and should not be allowed to return. But how much enthusiasm there was for going far in the opposite direction, of pressing forward the revolution in social responsibility which the war had brought about, was impossible to gauge, and would

only be known when peace itself was finally won. And this would not happen until the German armies had been so squeezed between the Allies advancing from the west and the Russians from the east that they, and their political rulers, had bowed in unconditional surrender to the liberating powers.

In the autumn of 1944, the nature of the peacetime government was to some extent an academic question. Although the Allies were advancing across Europe, the Germans counter-attacked and offered strong resistance. Victory was coming, but very slowly. What was certain was that an Allied victory would bring no relaxation of the effort the farming community would have to make in the immediate post-war years to keep Britain fed.

For an unspecified period of time, Europe, too,

would need feeding, and there was no prospect of European farming building up its livestock holding, and thus being able to supply Britain in turn with her pre-war quantities of condensed milk, bacon, cheese and eggs, for many years to come. The Allied farming communities would be in the position of having to rebuild European agriculture, as her bombed cities had to be rebuilt, by supplying machinery, fertilisers and seeds – all commodities in which supplies were difficult to come by for home production alone.

A further strain on British supplies would be the ending of Lend-Lease agreements with the United States, under which vast amounts of American military and civil equipment had been shipped across the Atlantic for use in Britain, on deferred terms of payment. A huge industrial export drive was going to have to take place for Britain to earn foreign exchange to begin to repay some of the vast debts she had incurred during the war. Much of Britain's foreign investment holding had been sold off during the war to provide cash and materials for war production. The income of foreign currency which these investments had produced was thus seriously depleted, and the deficit could only be made up by reconstructing Britain's

export industry. The custom had to be rebuilt, and so did the means of production, since virtually the entire industrial machine which Britain possessed had been directed towards the production of arms, military equipment and basic goods for home consumption. It was estimated that Britain would have to export nearly 75 per cent more than she did before the war, to pay for a level of imports no higher than the pre-war figure.

Imports had to be cut to the barest essentials: home food production therefore had to be maintained at its high level, and, whether the war ended in 1945 or not, the harvests of 1945 and 1946 had to be planned a year and eighteen months ahead. There was a hope that if peace came in 1945, the national diet, nutritious enough but, in general, unvarying and not always entirely palatable, could be broadened to include the common foodstuffs, meat, eggs, bacon and dairy products which were so hard to come by in the cities

World Farmers Unite to Defeat Hunger *below* and *right* Here a new British potato-planting machine, operated by German prisoners-of-war, is examined by Canadian farmers looking into technological developments of the wartime years.

during the worst years of the war. The cheapest way to increase the output of these products was to use what little foreign exchange was available to buy animal foodstuffs from abroad and breed the animals in Britain. For the harvest of 1945 the acreage under oats and other animal fodder crops was increased at the expense of the wheat crop, in order to provide extra fodder for the growing livestock herds that were planned. In January 1945, rations were increased for pigs, poultry and heifer calves, and a price review in February 1945 held out further inducements to farmers to shift into a greater proportion of livestock to arable farming than they had maintained throughout the war.

The farming community complied with the plan and the additional problem of a wet autumn in 1944 meant that the area of farmland planted with corn was diminished by almost three quarters of a million acres. Pigs, poultry and cattle grew in number; the prices for milk, fat stock and eggs were all raised during 1945. The acreage grant for wheat and rye was reduced and the price for potatoes and sugar-beet increased to maintain the emphasis of production on the latter two crops.

The decisions of the first half of 1945, with the Allies moving ever more surely towards Berlin and the downfall of the Third Reich, looked ahead to 1946, when it was hoped that the compulsory direction of farmers' output could be dispensed with; that the momentum of the present co-peration within the industry could be maintained by using the price mechanism to direct the overall balance of the output of British farms. Victory in Europe, on 7 May 1945, was welcomed by the feeling in British farming that the balance of their agriculture and the level of production was beginning to come right for a thriving rural industry to make a valuable and essential contribution to Britain in peacetime.

The celebrations of VE-Day were not long over when the Ministry of Agriculture began to be worried about the level of foodstuffs available in the country to feed the larger numbers of animals. Huge amounts of grain had had to be sent into Europe, where much of the agricultural land, particularly in the north, had been severely damaged. European farming was barely functioning at half its pre-war level. To make up the shortfall the Government looked to the United States and Canada, but in anticipation of the end of the war

the numbers of livestock had risen even more rapidly in the north American continent, and the animal foodstuffs were being consumed rather than exported.

The new Government of Britain, a Labour administration led by Clement Attlee, faced an increasingly severe situation. The autumn of 1945 brought the news that there were not enough cereals in the Allied granaries to feed all the animals that were being raised. At the same time fears for grain harvests in India and South Africa proved all too well founded, as prolonged droughts turned both countries' crops into national disasters. In spite of the fact of famine writ large across the world's grain markets, the Government pressed on with the optimistic strategy of increasing ration allowances of animal foodstuffs, and reducing the grant to farmers who grew wheat.

But the facts would not be dodged. In early 1946 it was announced that the imports of animal cereals would be well below the planned levels. Animal foodstuff rations were suddenly and severely cut, to the levels of the most stringent period of the war. In July 1946 the Labour Government was forced to do what had been avoided even during the worst period of the Battle of the Atlantic – to ration flour and bread. Barely twelve months after VE-Day, the benefits of a world at peace seemed further away than they had done since the years of the Nazi triumphs.

No-one could doubt that the farming community had played their part, with far greater results even than the sterling efforts of their fathers during the First World War. The land was in good heart. Given the encouragement and the opportunity to invest in repair and renewal of their machinery, British farmers were poised to play a greater part in their country's economy than they had for the last hundred years. Yet the world they faced was a different one from that of 1918, when the clock had been turned back, and from that of 1938, when it was ticking, but very slowly. The scale had changed forever, and so had Britain's position in relation to the other nations of the world. Victorious, but diminished in wealth; mobilised and superbly organised, but very tired and in need of re-equipment; united through the shared adversity, but riven still with scarcely-concealed suspicions and prejudices, the British people sought to plan a new future for themselves, and their political leaders to create a new stability among the nations in concert with Britain's Allies. The political and economic task was one of a size and complexity never before attempted. For Britain's farming community, as for Britain's industry, a clear solution was vital. The answers are still being worked out.

WLA parade, in Leamington Spa, with floats symbolising the various aspects of the Land Girls' work, to raise money for the WLA Benevolent Fund.

Index

Acknowledgements

Although every effort has been made to trace the copyright owners of illustrations, this has not always proved possible. We apologise for any inadvertant neglect of copyright acknowledgment.

Beaverbrook Newspapers Ltd, 25; Mrs Lynda Bullmore, 80 (below right); J. H. Cookson, 69, 111; L. R. Denton, 120 (below); George W. F. Ellis, 4, 20 (above, below), 21, 22, 32–3 (above), 78 (below), 96, 97 (below), 110; *Farmers' Weekly*, 45; Mrs Ruth Ford, 32 (below left, below right), 94; Fox Photos, 42 (centre left, bottom left); General Foods Ltd, 99; J. Hardman, 86 (above); Imperial War Museum, 2–3, 30, 33 (above right), 46 (above, below), 49, 50, 51 (above), 52 (above), 53, 57, 61, 63 (below), 65, 66, 71, 74 (above), 78 (above), 80 (above), 90, 91 (above), 104, 109 (above, below), 118 (above left); Ford Jenkins, 52 (below), 70 (above), 116; *Kent Messenger*, 72 (below), 117; Mrs K. E. Kenward, 33 (below); London News Agency, 42–3 (below); *Luton News*, 29, 55 (above); Mid-Essex Reporting Agency, 75; Museum of English Rural Life, 1, 4–5 (centre), 5 (below), 6–7, 9, 13, 15 (above, below), 19 (above), 38 (above), 39, 41, 43 (above), 55 (below), 64, 77, 79, 82, 83, 85, 86 (below), 92–3, 105, 107, 113, 125; Plymouth Central Library, 118 (above right), 119; *Punch*, 51 (below), 56 (above), 81 (below right), 98; Radio Times Hulton Picture Library, 10, 11, 12 (below), 14, 16, 17, 19 (below), 28, 31 (above, below), 34, 35, 37, 42 (above right), 44, 56 (below), 58, 59 (above, below), 60, 67, 70 (below), 76, 87 (above), 89, 91 (below), 95, 99 (below), 100 (above, below), 101, 102 (above), 103, 108, 114, 115, 118 (below), 120 (above), 122, 123; *Railway Gazette*, 27 (below); Mrs Florence Roe, 81 (below left); Ryvita Co. Ltd, 38 (below); Sport and General Press Agency, 42 (above left), 74 (below), 84, 97 (above); Syndication International, 26, 47, 54, 103 (below); Thomson Regional Newspapers, 12 (above), 112 (left); John Topham, 121; Bertram Urne, 112 (right); Watford Central Library, 6 (above), 18 (below), 62, 63 (above), 72 (above), 81 (above); Weetabix Ltd, 87 (below); Women's Royal Voluntary Service, 6 (below), 27 (above), 32 (above left, centre left), 33 (centre right), 80 (below left).

The authors would like to thank the following for their help in the preparation of this book:
Mrs P. M. Chadwell, S. J. Coates, Mrs M. E. Johnson, G. A. Marsh, R. H. Newitt, K. Paterson, Mrs J. Patinson, S. C. Savage, Mrs E. M. Wakely.

Bibliography

We owe a debt for factual material to the following books:

Farmers' Rights Association, *Living Casualties,* 1950

Fleming, P., *Invasion 1940,* Hart-Davis, 1957

Fordham, M., *The Land and Life,* Rural Reconstruction Association, 1942

Graves, C., *Life Line,* Heinemann, 1941

Lafitte, F., *The Internment of Aliens,* Penguin, 1940

Longmate, N., *How We Lived Then,* Hutchinson, 1971

— *The Real Dad's Army,* Arrow, 1974

Murray, K. A. H., *Agriculture,* HMSO/Longmans, 1955

Orr, J. B. & Lubbock, D., *Feeding the People in Wartime,* Macmillan, 1940

Orwin, C. S., *Problems of the Countryside,* Cambridge University Press, 1945

— *Speed the Plough,* Penguin, 1942

Panter-Downes, M., *London War Notes,* Longmans, 1972

Ritchie, C., *The Siren Years,* Macmillan, 1974

Street, A. G., *From Dusk till Dawn,* Blandford, 1947

Sykes, F., *This Farming Business,* Faber & Faber, 1944

Taylor, A. J. P., *English History 1914–1945,* Oxford University Press, 1965

Turner, E. S., *The Phoney War on the Home Front,* Michael Joseph, 1961

West, V. Sackville-, *The Women's Land Army,* Michael Joseph, 1940

— *Country Notes in Wartime,* Hogarth Press, 1940

Whetham, E., *British Farming 1939–1949,* Nelson, 1952